Flying Lessons

Angela Kari Gutwein

Black Rose Writing | Texas

ISBN: 978-1-68433-224-3
PUBLISHED BY BLACK ROSE WRITING
www.blackrosewriting.com

Printed in the United States of America
Suggested Retail Price (SRP) $18.95

Flying Lessons is printed in Chaparral Pro
Front Cover Photo courtesy of Kris Smith
Back Cover Photo courtesy of Audrey Helbling, https://mnprairieroots.com/
Illustrations courtesy of Nixdaly Riojas
Edited by Lisa Bell and Beth Knudson
Author Photo courtesy of Kris Smith
Song: *I Love You, Lord*, Words and music by Laurie Klein

For Mom

With tears, I dedicate this book to Mom. She loved her babies. When they placed me, her firstborn, on her chest, she said, "I am complete."

Mom, you teased us. You pushed us. You held us and loved us. Your touch melted me. Your smile soothed me. And your presence strengthened me.

You taught me to love and give and respect.

You demonstrated the significance and beauty of working in the soil. Together we would choose vegetable and flower varieties sometimes, just because.

You raised the four us all by yourself and placed on me more than my fair share of the responsibility.

Your source of strength, an unwavering surety in the Love of Christ, held you and supported you. I watched you create a home that was greater than scraping by and grew to value hard work and tenacity. If no is the answer, ask a different question. If you fall, get up and find a new way.

But the most important lesson...

Life is not survival. It is not a battle to be conquered or a race to be won. Life is meant to be lived. Fully. Completely. Without fear.

A young woman battles with guilt and fear following a fatal car accident. Longing to give up, she must uncover the secret to trusting God through the pain and grief.

Will she learn to fly?

To my Reader

This is a deeply personal story, but I believe the more personal, the more universal and communally rich it becomes. You may progress through many emotions as you walk alongside me, waking up the demons within. I challenge you to face them.

Trauma unravels our true being, affecting our ability to create and embody the glory of God.

It's experienced and hard to squeeze into the straitjacket of verbal expression. It is visceral, requiring non-verbal cues. It begs performance and repeated telling to heal.

Trauma takes us to the very limits of language, where we cross into the threshold of silence.

Take your time with this book. There are four sections: the egg, the eaglet, the fledgling and the eagle. The fledgling is especially difficult. Be kind to yourself. Put it down and let it digest. I'll be here when you get back.

Eleven brief pauses, inserted within, will keep us grounded and present. The questions will assist in the healing process. Seek out choice souls to hold it with you. Dogs work.

These eleven flying lessons, listed at the end, are for the suffering and for those who want to love them well when there is nothing to do.

Breathe and turn the page.

Flying Lessons

Part One

The Egg

Surrounded by a protective shell, a new life develops until it can survive on its own.

I will put thee in a cleft of the rock,
and will cover thee with My hand
Until I have passed by.
Exodus 33:22

1
My Prison

Smoke seeps through cracks in the bedroom door, and the familiar sting of Marlboro Lights overwhelms my senses. Not again. I squeeze my nose together. That smell means so much more. Focus. Block it out. Your Orbital Dynamics homework will not do itself.

Great grandma's quilts are still rolled up and stacked in the corner from the last time. I press them up against the bottom of the door, but it's already in the room, assaulting my senses. Pulling at my...

Focus.

To repair the satellite's telemetry system, Dave readies himself for another spacewalk. The spring-loaded launching device gives him an initial speed of one meter per second and the satellite is drifting away from the space station at two meters per second.

He's smoking. A lot. That means he's also drinking. If I just focus on my homework, it won't impact me this time. Maybe if I stay locked in this room, I can ignore what's going on downstairs.

Mom and I love to be together, so this room is where we work. Mom set up her sewing machine on one side, while I have my desk on the other, but it has changed hands many times over the years as one-by-one we all moved out to attend college. It's the smallest of the three bedrooms, so it started as the kids' bedroom. That's what we call Ursula and Micah, the youngest of us four siblings. Teressa and I each got our own. Ursula moved into mine when I left for college. Three years later, Micah followed suit.

I wind my way through the quilt pieces from Mom's latest project, blanketing the floor, to the window. Looking down into the backyard, the half-frozen waterfall trickles over the rocks into the swimming pool. Lights bounce through steam rising off the black pool mimicking one carved out of the Rocky Mountains. The idyllic scene distracts me for a few seconds, until I imagine the scene playing out downstairs.

No, no, no. Closing my eyes, I don't need to imagine. I know. I've lived it many times over.

My homework! Returning to my desk, I rub my eyes, attempting to scrub out the knowledge.

The total mass of Dave and his maneuvering unit is three hundred kilograms. What is the magnitude of the thrust required to intercept the satellite?

Sounds are muffled, but mom's pain still finds its way into my heart.

Focus!

What is his velocity when he reaches the satellite as referenced to the satellite but observed by the space station?

I can't focus.

Even upstairs behind the closed door, I can't escape. The house is big enough to hide from the turmoil, but the muffled noises and diluted smells make escape impossible. My stepfather, Robert, is in one of his moods. He brings a heaviness to the house even in his best moments.

This is not one of his best.

With the smoke, my mom's enduring pain weaves its way up the stairs and through the cracks.

C'mon Gala, tune it out. Instead, I sink deep into my own world. A prison. A prison I love, and I hate. I'm protected, but I can't breathe. The walls press in. I can't stay in this artfully crafted prison all night. When Mom's in here, this little room opens, warm air rushes and swirls.

To reach her, I must open the door.

Pushing the quilts away with my foot, I crack it just wide enough to suck through. Holding my breath, I slide out, promptly closing the door behind me in a vain attempt to keep the smoke out. Nothing is filtered or muffled or diluted anymore. My pupils quickly shrink to pinholes as they are hit by the light coming off the chandelier just on the other side of the railing. Every light in the house is on. Like the scene in the backyard, lights mingle with smoke. Not so idyllic.

Looking to the left, then to the right. I reacquired my bedroom when I moved back to finish a second degree. It's down the hall, and the bathroom to the right.

No, I need to see. My imagination could be worse. The cloud of smoke gets thicker as I make my way down the stairs, winding around the foyer.

Under the staircase, Mom and Robert stand in the cramped hallway leading to the master suite, bedroom and office. With a cigarette in one hand and a bottle of Moët in the other, he demands a copy of her nursing license. Football commentary roars out of the television in the bedroom. Nicotine and alcohol laced sweat seeps out of his pores. My nose crinkles against his noxious body odor.

He leans in to grab her arm. I can't watch this; my imagination was spot on. I turn on my heel to the other side of the foyer, which opens into the front sitting room, but I see it all unfolding in my brain as if I had eyes in the back of my head.

Equipped with a Disklavier, Mom's glossy white, baby-grand player-piano bangs out Bach. Zeek's fluffy white tail ruffles the sheer curtains framing the bay window. The grandfather clock brings in the ten o'clock hour, switching my attention towards the living room. Walking past Robert, his alcohol-glazed eyes look through me. Rage spilling out.

Empty beer and champagne bottles litter the living room floor. Tables, chairs, couches, fireplace mantle, kitchen counters. All available surfaces covered with dirty dishes. None of this was here at the beginning of the evening. Partly congealed, orange grease crusts around ashes and half-eaten food. Butts float in half-empty beer bottles and champagne glasses. The living room television belts out another station with more sports commentary.

Looking back, I rest on her eyes. Sadness not fear or anger.

Drunk-angry, Robert blathers. "Unauthorized entry into the office." He motions to grab her arm, forgetting the champagne glass in his hand. Moët sloshes over the top.

"I'm your wife. How can you call it unauthorized entry?" Backing away, the wall stops her six inches from him. Champagne splashes down her leg.

"You take things," he fires back.

She sees me. Her face is red and swollen.

Our eyes speak without words. *It's okay, Gala. I'll survive.*

Survival mode. Her whole life she's been living in survival mode. Oh, I love when she calls me Gala. Short for Angela, pronounced ahn-GAY-lah.

Did he hit her, knock her around, burn her with any of those cigarettes? With a cursory glance, I can't find any fresh evidence.

When will she stop? Breathe. Have time for me? But I really don't expect that.

I believe the lie. I do not need.

Defeat drags down her shoulders. But I do need her. Soon it will change, if I'm just patient. We will get through this. A time very soon, I just know it, she will come out the other side. Her eyes will open. Fresh air will fill her lungs. She will, we will survive. Then she will see me deep down and say, "Precious Gala, I'm so proud to be your mother."

C'mon, Mom. Fight. I need you to fight. Or leave. Why are we still here? How do we get out?

Preparations began months ago when she told me she wanted to be sure I would be able to stay here until I graduated. Not without her, I can't stay without her. How can she even think about leaving me behind? The walls press in, sinking deeper into my prison.

A few days later, I found a scrap of paper saying, *For the kids*. It had the few expensive items that belong to her, not Robert. Last week she took me to the bank and signed over her account, explaining she didn't want Robert to have access. What's her plan? Does it include me? I put on my brave face and wait.

Changes are coming.

It sits just under the surface. She wants out. To be free of Robert. But she fears the stigma. The scarlet letter. Another marriage ending in another divorce.

I fear she desires freedom from it all. Is she tired of me, too? Do I exhaust her? I've tried so hard to be small. Not to need. To carry as much of her burden as possible.

She scoops up a dirty t-shirt to dry off her legs and slips around him. She motions with her head and her eyes towards the living room. At her cue, I turn, leaving Robert in our dust. The eyes in the back of my head see him stumble around, eventually retiring to his bedroom.

We silently clean the endless mess from Robert's temper tantrum. There really isn't anything to be said. This isn't the first time. After thirty minutes,

Mom releases me with a hug.

"Go finish your homework, honey. I'll take care of the rest."

I tiptoe upstairs. With a thud, the prison bars lock down behind me. I can focus. Now, that I've seen.

It takes four pages of green engineering paper to calculate the thrust required to intercept the satellite, the time it takes Dave to get there and what his velocity will be once he makes it. Ah, the safe world of aerospace engineering. Questions number two and three involve a mass on a smooth surface, forces acting with and against it. Each requires two more pages of calculations and three plots. I label and number each page, staple it together and load up my backpack for the next day's classes.

Squeezing out into the hallway, I tiptoe from the bathroom to my bedroom. Lights still shine bright, and the smoke hangs heavy. Behind the closed door, I tune it out, turn on my noise machine and fall asleep. A restless, uneasy sleep, but at least I can't hear him.

Three AM, 24 January 2001

Robert corners his wife against the kitchen counter. Janet's heart sinks, solidifying into a tangible mass of fear and grief. Drunk and furious, he leans heavy against her. Champaign-sticky thighs peel apart, as she tries to rotate out, but he plants his feet. Sharp laminate corners dig into Janet's back. Exhaling, her eyes drop. Robert's arms form a barrier on either side.

"How are Jack Caffey's legs? Bitch! What do you think would happen if somebody beat the hell out of Jack Caffey? Do you think he'd ever want to fuck you?" He presses play with the same accusations. Different day. Different guy. Same story.

The vicious words penetrate past her callused heart. There's nothing she can say. He's not going to believe or hear her. He imagines her lovers spread out all over Jasper County.

"You're nuts." She musters up all her strength and pushes past him to the sink. He would never have the courage to do it himself, but he could hire someone.

He sinks his fingers into her bicep, wrenching her around. "Don't turn away from me. I'm talking to you." Blood vessels burst; fresh bruises show their ugly head.

He yanks the glass from her hand. Dripping in hot soapy suds, it slips through his fingers, slams into the cabinet and shatters on her bare feet, blood bubbling out around speared shards.

"See what you do." His face inches from hers, spit flies into her eyes.

She blinks, pushing her hand against his chest. Frozen against the kitchen counter, she can't move without cutting herself.

He looks down at the shards covering her bare feet, leaning in, the fire in his eyes penetrating past the alcohol-induced stupor.

In a slow sinister whisper. "I am not cleaning that up."

He stomps-staggers out, struggling to connect his feet to the floor, glass crunching underfoot.

With a dish towel, she clears a swath. Soapy shards mopped up and in the trash, she can sit and pluck the rest from her skin.

She retrieves the first aid kit from their bathroom cabinet.

Robert rolls out of his stupor.

"Where's my tape? I'm not leaving here without it. Where did you put it?" He closes the gap between them.

"What tape?" She moves towards the door.

Clinching a screwdriver in his right hand, he steps in.

Oh, my god, what is he planning to do with that?

"Don't get funny with me. Now, you're going to tell me where it is, or one of us isn't going to be here."

He lifts the screwdriver, motioning towards her neck.

"I could use this on you. What would you do then?"

He's going to kill her. Her body shakes as grief and fear war inside. How does she get out? Angela's upstairs. Does she wake her? Do they run?

"You're a whore. There's only two other women I've met like you. Why did you marry me? You just take take take..."

That's a very good question. How? Why? This is not me.

They fell in love, at least she thought so.

Robert treated her like a queen and exposed her children to exotic restaurants and expensive gifts. For eight years, they dated. She didn't go into this easily. Her first marriage ended in divorce, and her four kids were always her priority.

Still she waited until one fateful morning, a phone call announced the death of her first husband. Hijackers shot him in Brazil!

She heard whispers of mental illness. Bipolar disorder. He had a wandering eye and a wandering soul. Young co-eds in tube tops and bell bottoms were his specialty. She was the responsible one, the bread-winner, the parent. He dragged his young family all around the country in pursuant of his next college degree or business scheme until she put it to a stop.

Janet wanted to be cared for, loved and pursued.

Robert did until the exotic restaurant outings turned sinister as an angry drunk emerged. Her home is a prison. His mood never predictable. Car keys confiscated at his whim. Paranoid, jealous accusations color the once-upon-a-time fairy tale.

She pulls herself back to the present. Back to this man, her husband, holding a screwdriver. Spitting out threats and accusations.

How is this my life?

She stands toe-to-toe. Shoulders back. Chest out. Without a word, he slumps over. Thump. The screwdriver hits the ground. Robert returns to his bed. Janet retires to an upstairs bedroom and locks the door.

2
Lonely Red Octagon

Beep... beep... beep...

I fling my arm up above my head, slamming down the button. Silence. Immediately sliding back under the warm covers, I snuggle the down comforter under my chin and curl up for eight more minutes of sleep.

Beep... beep... beep...

The eight minutes feels like one as the alarm jolts me out of my restless sleep. Memories of the previous evening flood in. My stomach turns, slathering fear into my muscles. Paralyzed, but safe if I stay hidden under the tight and toasty.

A need to succeed overrides the fear, injecting adrenalin through those fear-paralyzed muscles. I love my aerospace classes, and I'm good at it. This flipped out, messed up, crazy situation will not stop me. The red, LED numbers tell me I'm late, popping me out of bed.

Sliding up the shades, the soft, blue moonlight is perfect, and just enough light.

Opening the bedroom door, the sting of Marlboro Lights still lingers. I pause, fear threatens to drown, but the assault to the rest of my senses is gone. It's cold but pleasantly dark and quiet. One small Tiffany lamp illuminates the hallway. Tense shoulders soften, knowing Mom did that for me.

I have room to breathe, space to be me, albeit a wary me.

Tiptoeing down the stairs, can't wake the sleeping giant.

The bottles and the butts and the beers. Evidence of Robert's temper tantrum has disappeared. Mom finished everything after I tiptoed up to my prison. The kitchen sparkles, countertops bare, everything in its rightful spot. All is back to normal.

Another tiny lamp illuminates the kitchen in a gentle, warm light.

How does she do that? Make everything good and safe. I rest in her, and the fear sits in the background, ready when I need it.

We're late and don't have time to make our lunches. She mixes up some oatmeal for us to eat on the way.

The dreary January morning echoes our hearts.

It's six, and we're finally off.

We've been making this trip every day for the last two years when mom got a job at a small Call-a-Nurse company.

.   .   .   .   .

"Try this. It's so comfortable." Mom's eyes sparkle as she rotates the chair counterclockwise. Sitting on a brand-new, clear, plastic mat, it flies around. She halts its motion, poised for me. She looks down at the mat, then up at me. *Cool, huh?* Her eyes say it all. I smile in response. Words without words flow between us with even less effort than the flying chair.

It sinks into my weight, comfort and support perfectly balanced.

"And look." Practically dancing as, she slips the headset over my ears. Her fingertips tenderly brush across my cheeks, down my neck and out through my hair. So much love communicated in such a common motion.

"A headset." The word punctuated with a smile. A smile that could heat the sun.

It's not the chair or headset. She's finally getting her own life. She's done her time in the local hospital's emergency room and in Robert's family practice, located across the street from the hospital and two blocks from home. This small world under Robert's influence seems impenetrable. Is this her way out?

A job in the big city of Lafayette, Indiana.

The office is a few miles from Purdue, where I'm getting my second college degree.

Every day we escape. Every day we take turns driving the thirty minutes. Every day we return.

•   •   •   •   •

Not as tired as her, I get in the driver's seat.

As I back out, she hands me a spoonful of oatmeal. I return the empty spoon and put the car into drive. The tires spin and then catch hold.

Driving past the first side road, "I guess we'll take the main road today. There's a little too much snow, don't you think?" The words feel like thoughts, but float out in a soft whisper.

She nods, the spoon clanks against the little glass bowl. Her face says it all. We're not going to talk this morning.

South Iliff Drive dead-ends two blocks later at State Road 114, Jasper County Hospital directly ahead. To our left, Robert's office is dark. Once upon a time, Mom would already be at work typing out insurance claims, readying rooms, counting pills, pulling the days' charts.

Turning right, 114 is clear. Clear of snow. Clear of ice. And clear of any sign of life. In less than a half mile, we cross the Iroquois River. It flows but the banks are frozen. Our turn is just ahead. Another right.

The spoon clanks with the glass, and I swallow more oatmeal. This is just a country road, but it's paved and we're on it for two miles, when it jogs to the left, then right, kicking us out onto County Road 380.

A whisper thin layer of fresh snow blows along the top three inches of flat Indiana farmland.

I have driven 380 thousands of times at all hours of the day and night and in all types of weather. It's so familiar, I could drive it blindfolded. A fifteen-mile straight line interrupted at the halfway mark by a lone stop sign. Frozen, rutted soil sails by. Thousands of corn stalks impale the ground surrounding us, cut down in the harvest three months ago.

The melancholy oatmeal exchange continues. She knows when I'm ready for the next bite before I do. Words without words.

Five hundred feet away, a quiet intersection with a lonely, red, octagon prompts me to slow. Mom leans forward, placing the empty bowl on the floorboard. The clanking spoon makes one last utterance as it pops out of the bowl, settling on the floorboard. She glances up, then flies back colliding against her seat.

Our eyes meet as she flings her arm against my chest. Blinding light besieges me.

Fear. Raw fear. In her eyes.

My foot flies to the left. Crushes the brake, plunging it through the floorboard.

Mom!

3
Where's Mom?

I wake in a dark hospital room. Just the indirect lights behind me illuminate. A nurse walks over to the IV stand. Two bags hang, a big, bulging clear one and another, sucked dry, yellow liquid filling the creases. She swaps it with a full one, then changes out her gloves from the boxes affixed to the wall. Without looking up, she gently lifts my arm, reads the band and takes my pulse.

"Where's Mom?"

Startled, she drops my arm and smiles. "Oh honey, you're awake. Just a minute, I'll go get the doctor."

Minutes pass in silence until the room fills with doctors and nurses. The overhead lights pop on. I'm surrounded. They move too fast for me to follow. The air buzzes with their excitement.

"Where's Mom?"

A penlight shines into my eyes while someone else puts a cuff around my right arm. "It's okay, Angela, you were in a car accident." The clinical voice rebounds in my foggy brain.

What? We were eating oatmeal. Now, I'm... Oh no, my homework?

"Where's my backpack? Did someone turn in my homework?"

"I'm Doctor Ross. You're in the ICU at Methodist Hospital in Indianapolis. You were airlifted here early this morning." The army in my room poke and prod focusing on my left arm.

Slow down. I don't understand. Mom?

"Why isn't she in the bed next to me? Is she okay?"

"Can you feel that?" Doctor Ross pokes my arm in several places.

Stop. Please tell me. Then I can focus on this arm.

Before I can answer, another doctor asks me to move my fingers. *Of course, see.* I lift my head to watch the fingers wave but the wrist and arm... *why doesn't it move?* I try harder. It remains motionless. *What's going on?*

Doctor Ross continues. "The bicep and deltoid of your left arm is paralyzed. We still don't know if this is permanent."

Um, what? Okay, that's fine. I crunch my eyes tight. *What was I saying? Oh yeah.* "Where's Mom?"

"Your brother will be here in a few hours." A nurse replies.

"Is she okay?"

There's a deep burn in my right arm. *Whoa, what was that?* My head flies around to the right as a nurse removes a needle. Everything fades away.

· · · · ·

Micah drops the phone, slumping to the ground. His head spins. His project? Mom? Ang? His class project, worth fifty percent of the semester grade. Maybe his professor will give him an extension? Another phone call interrupts his thoughts.

"Aunt Quinnell's on her way to pick you up. She'll be there in two hours."

"Okay." He fumbles with the cordless phone, eventually giving up as it rolls out of his hand. The headset buzzes.

He can't wait, jumping to his feet.

· · · · ·

My eyes open. Micah sits in the far corner, slumped over cupping his head in his hands.

"Micah?"

"Hi Ang. How are you feeling?" He walks over, his shoulders droop with fatigue.

"Hey. Have you talked to Mom?"

A nurse walks in. "Angela, can you tell me your name?"

You just said it.

I ignore her and turn towards Micah.

"Teressa will be here in the morning." Micah leans over, kissing me on the forehead.

There's that deep burn again.

·   ·   ·   ·   ·

Teressa unlocks the front door, turning sideways to fit through. She's due in eight weeks. Her first. Cole shifts his weight, leaning against the far wall. She sees her husband's concern, but it doesn't register. She just wants to tell him about the incredible find she acquired at *Once Upon a Child*.

"Hey Cole, what are you doing home? Look what I just..." She stops, suddenly noticing her in-laws. "Mama Di?"

His parents sit quietly on the couch.

"Come over here and sit down." Cole deftly closes the distance between them before she can take a breath.

Her smile drops instantly. Bags thump to the floor. He reaches out to her just as she straightens her arms against his chest.

"What's going on? You're scaring me."

"C'mon T, sit next to me. Something's happened." Mama Di reaches out, placing a hand on the couch.

She pushes past Cole and chooses the chair to the right of Mama Di.

"There's been an accident." Cole sits next to his mother, turning towards his wife. "Angela's in the hospital. Her arm is paralyzed. They say she ran a stop sign."

"And Mom? Were they together?"

·   ·   ·   ·   ·

My eyes open to the same room. Same bed. Same large paneled windows. So bright. Too bright. *Is it the next day?* Blinding bright. My head turns to escape the light. The rooftops are covered by a fresh foot of snow. I rub my eyes. Only one hand reaches my face. *What's wrong with that arm?* The fingers on my left hand strain, but the arm just lays there. *That doctor said something about... Mommy?!?*

"How do you feel?" Aunt Marsha asks.

Several family members come in. More red eyes but they still refuse to tell me where she is. *Is she...?*

With more of the same questions, a nurse puts a cuff around my arm.

"Okay, Sweetie, what's your name and date of birth?" She lifts my wrist to read the band.

Not again. At least she didn't give me the answer this time. "Angela. Nine. Twenty-six. Seventy-two."

"Good, where are you?"

You better give me some answers. "The hospital in Indianapolis." Just trying to get this part done. But I need to know.

"Where's Mom?"

The burn. But before everything fades away, I overhear Marsha and a nurse talking in the far corner.

"She needs to know." Says the nurse.

"Robert doesn't want us to..." Marsha's voice fades away.

Another day. That same bright sun reflects off the snow-covered rooftops.

The room is quiet and empty save two aunts. Marsha and Janet are my dad's sisters. Well, he wasn't a dad. He took off when I was eight. To me, he's Mark, not Dad. Twelve years ago, Marsha told me about Mark's death.

Is this happening?

.   .   .   .   .

The school bus drops us off, and the kids race up the hill, leaving me in the dust. At sixteen, I can't be bothered by such antics. The phone rings, as I step through the back door.

I push past them to answer, but Micah slips by. I yank the handset from him before he can say anything.

"Hello."

"Hi honey. This is Aunt Marsha. Is your mom home?" Her voice cracks.

"She'll be home in a few minutes. What's wrong?"

"Something's happened with your dad." Her voice breaks off. She's crying. Pressure wells up in my chest. *He's dead, I just know it.* Heat swells my cheeks. I push it away. *Maybe it's a good thing. Now, Mom and Robert can get married. Now, I can have a dad.*

Marsha's broken voice talks about hijackers and gunshots. I piece the bits together.

Micah pulls at me. "Who is it? Who's on the phone? C'mon, Ang, I want to talk."

Mom walks through the door, as I shake free of the little parasite. The phone cord snakes across the living room, into the kitchen. "Hey Mom. Here." Handing her the phone, my feelings are all over the place. *He died. Good news, right? But... Oh, I don't know.* "It's Marsha."

The kids gather around me. "What happened?"

"It's about Mark. He died, so now Mom can get married." I tell my siblings our father just died with a smile on my face.

A smile.

Teressa locks herself in the bathroom. *Oops, maybe that wasn't the right thing to say.* Taking their cue from me, the kids celebrate.

Mom hangs up the phone. She's crying. *Oh, maybe this isn't such a good thing.* She gives us the details. We learn he was visiting Aunt Gail in Argentina, and his bus was hijacked. They shot him four times in the back.

She sobs behind her bedroom door. I stand, stunned, in the hallway. The kids dance around me, running back and forth between the kitchen and their bedroom. Audible tears from the two closed doors.

•   •   •   •   •

I ask again. "Is Mom okay?"

They just look at me, never breaking eye contact.

"Where is she?"

Tears pour out.

"Is Mom dead?"

The color drops out of their cheeks. Then...

Their heads nod.

"No!" I turn to the left trying to get away. *Where's my door to cry behind?* In a flash, I turn back thinking this can't be true. "Is it a joke? Are you kidding?"

Who would play such a cruel joke?

Their eyes scream confirmation. Mom's gone.

It starts out benign. Just a slight discomfort. I can almost ignore it until without much fanfare or permission. It takes root and grows. It grows offshoots into every corner of my being. The tentacles are alive, burning the grief deeper. It is relentless, pressing hard, invading. My ribs feel as though they are ripping apart. Stretching and tearing.

My elevated heart rate sets off the machines. Buzzers and beeps fill the room as wide-eyed nurses come rushing in. Marsha and Janet jump to their feet. The overhead lights pop on. I lose control.

I breathe hard for less oxygen. My chest heaves. Up. Down. Up. Down. The air stops at the massive lump that was once my heart. Burning, lava tears blind me. Mucus fills my sinuses, dripping and leaking everywhere. Parched lips. I can't swallow past my swollen tongue. My heart, the actual muscle, feels twice its normal size. It beats in my eyes, my ears, my head.

Stop. Please slow down. I need. I need. I need to stop. Breathe. Instead of filling with oxygen, the tentacles invade and burn into my lungs.

My jaw tightens like a vise. Swollen arteries beat in my ears. Sweat beads in the small of my back, heat radiating up my shoulder blades and into my head. It feels like a fifty-pound bosu ball, crushing the pillow it rests on, tight like a headache but not. My eyes have nothing left to leak out. The lids are sticky and impossible to close.

Nurses look past me to the monitor.

Lifting my hand, my right hand, the only hand that works, to my eyes, I force them closed. I force the pain inside.

With every breath, I go deeper. The shell wraps around. *Breathe.* Pressing fingers hard against my eyelids, I'm sealed in. Safe. Alone. *Breathe.* I cannot love again. Nothing can touch me here.

The tentacles recede. *Breathe.* The heat dissipates. *Breathe.* My fingers soften, sliding off my eyes, down my face and rest on my chest.

My eyes open.

I laugh inside at the commotion I just caused. *Don't worry, guys. That cardiac event was just my heart exploding.* The nurses realize what I just learned and bow their heads, backing out of the room.

The last one brushes the light switch down. Marsha and Janet slip in close, embracing me.

4
I Need Her

Pulling the Velcro apart, I slip off the sling. My arm instantly plops down to my side. Marsha helps me out of my gown. Is this what shock feels like? I'm dazed, disconnected, out of it, not even in my body. I don't care about anything. The funeral is today, and I'm still in the ICU. The decision is made. I must attend my mother's funeral. Robert's a doctor, and I'm released into his care.

My cousin Melinda turns on the shower. Propping me up, Marsha and Melinda wash my hair. I can't put on my bra, tie my shoes or do my hair. Shouldn't this be humiliating?

They load me up in a wheelchair and push me to the car. Whoosh. The winter air bursts over me as the automatic door opens. My eyes close, but my body is motionless, limp. Not even the bitter cold warrants a reaction. Everything is being done for me. To me. I don't have control of anything. I'm not present enough to care. The nurse or whoever he is, locks the wheels and lifts, rotating me around and into the backseat.

The countryside has been covered by the constant deluge of snow over the last few days. I spend the next three hours lost inside my head mesmerized by the soft white blanket covering the world.

The car door opens, jolting me to reality. The winter air rushes in, and my feet sink into the cold white fluff.

Uncle Paul leans in over me and pulls out my crutch. Sliding his arm under mine, he expertly lifts me up out of the car and places the stick under my right arm. After a few precarious steps in the icy, slushy mess, he takes it back and steadies me himself.

We cross the road and enter through the side door. Trinity United

Methodist Church. All eyes turn to me. Back on dry ground, I lean on the crutch. I see my mother's friends, brothers and sister, people from all areas of her life and mine. Our lives are one. Now we've been yanked apart, leaving behind a deep chasm.

"Come here." Robert grabs my elbow and leads me to a table with pictures and trinkets from my mother's way too short life. Eighteen years ago, he came into our lives while Mom was working as the head emergency room nurse at the county hospital, and the four of us shuttled from one babysitter to the next.

Looking past them all, I try to turn to the front of the room, but wobble and trip over the crutch under my right shoulder. Someone catches me.

"I want to go up there." Pointing to the front of the room with my head. All I want is Mom. I'm led to the casket. Her arms are crossed over her chest. I'm too scared to touch her. The fear brings with it overwhelming grief. The lava tentacles invade once more. I'm frozen. Locked in place. Lost in time.

"It's time." The voice belongs to one of the funeral home workers addressing Robert.

It's time? I try to scream but nothing comes out.

A few others come over and close the casket. Mom locked inside.

Wait. No. I'm not ready. Grami glides her hand into mine, softly intertwining our fingers and leads me through the door, down a dark, narrow hallway to the sanctuary's anteroom.

No, please wait. Frantically turning my head every which way in search of that box, in search of my mommy.

Last time we were here, Mom and Robert got married. I was so excited to finally have a dad. Already a senior in high school, I was going to be a pre-med student at Indiana University, just like Robert. I'd been wearing the red and white sweatshirt with the big IU on the chest for three years. Pairing it with the matching red sweatpants. Robert bought me a chemistry set on my birthday that year and taught me how to use it.

The organ starts as my mom's siblings and mother are led into the sanctuary. I strain around. Where's the casket? Where's mom?

All that's left are my two little sisters, my baby brother and Robert. Like the wedding, I'm first. I'm the oldest. I've always been first. I've always been in charge.

Ah, finally the box. Directly in front of me. The shiny, wooden box with Mom locked inside. My heart rate slows, and I disappear into the past.

. . . . .

"Ursula's head is really bleeding. My boom box fell off the shelf, and there's this big gash on her head." I yell to Mom on the other end of the phone. "No, she didn't lose consciousness." Responding to her many questions.

"What I need you to do is put pressure on it until the bleeding stops. Then go to the medicine cabinet and get..." Mom continues with calm, clear instructions, reassuring me of her confidence in me. "I will be home as soon as I can. Just keep pressure on it and don't let her fall asleep."

I drop the blood-stained receiver and embrace my sister's head against my chest. It's going to take at least a half hour for Mom to get home. Why does she have to work so far away? I just need to get busy stopping this blood.

Still embraced against my chest, we stumble and trip over each other all the way down the hall and into the bathroom, leaving a trail of bloody footprints.

I turn on the faucet, half cold, half hot, and wait for the perfect temperature. Gently releasing my hands, her head arches under the water flow.

"Ang, that hurts."

"I know honey, but we need to clean it out. It'll be just a few more seconds. See, all done." I turn off the water. "Stay there while I get the towels, Okay?"

"Okay, thanks. I'm sorry."

"It's okay. Let's get you dried off."

"No, for going in your room."

Closing my eyes, I shake my head. My room. I had to carve out a corner of the playroom as "my room." I have too many siblings to get my own room. I staked my claim, and make sure everyone knows it. So much so this precious girl is gushing blood and apologizing for it.

Two hours later.

What's she been doing all this time? Doesn't she know, I need her? Mom bursts in ignoring the trail of sopping-bloody towels leading all the way down the hall, through the kitchen and into the bathroom. Ursula rests her head in my lap as we wait on the couch, eyes glued to the front door. Clumps of wet hair fall between my white knuckles.

Mom kneels in front of me, gently peeling away my fingers. With her touch, my shoulders instantly relax. Ah. I relax. I let go. Mom's here.

Removing the towel, she looks up. "That looks okay, Ang."

"How are you?" She asks cocking her head to look into Ursula's eyes.

Ursula just kinda moans, tears still wet her cheeks.

Mom opens the bag she just placed at my feet. My heart slows as she cleans the wound with betadine and finishes with Steri-Strips and gauze pads.

· · · · ·

The casket, my mom, continues her journey to the front of the room. Stop. Wait. I need you.

Robert steadies me as we are led to the front row. I sit down, leaning my crutch against the piano. It slides, in slow motion. I watch, just watch. Thud, crack, bang, tumbling to the ground. The full sanctuary, standing room only, is frozen in time. Nobody moves or says a word. My eyes slowly scan up from the ground. Black heels. Dress slacks. Bodies pushed together on long wooden pews. My high school French teacher looks into my eyes, touching my soul. Mrs. Jungbloode's presence is a strange comfort.

They sing a song or two. I stare at the closed casket just in front of me. I want Mommy. What happened? Is it my fault?

The service continues with some guy dressed in a white robe. The bright red stole drapes down to his knees. He talks about, I have no idea, but I'm pretty sure it's something in the Bible. Who is this guy? Did he know Mom? We didn't even go to this church anymore. This is Robert's church. Well actually his parents are members. That's what you do to look good. Do they even love Jesus?

I want to jump up and scream. *Stop. Don't you get it? I need my mom.*

David gets up and says some nice things about Mom. David and Robert are childhood friends. What about Mom's friends?

Robert puts his arm around me. I want to pull away, but I also want his comfort. I'm still angry with him but sink into his warmth. Just a few days ago he was yelling at us and pushing her around. I still don't know if he put those cigarettes out on her.

My attention returns to the service and David is sobbing. Sobbing. He can't talk anymore. Cole walks up to the lectern, places a gentle hand on his shoulder and takes over.

Wow, he did love her. He was her friend too.

A few more songs. The funeral is ending, my heart is racing. That guy gets back up, his bright red stole brushes against Mom's shiny box. In unison, the room stands. The wooden pews make a deep hallow sound. He closes the service with a prayer and benediction.

The mood changes. Small talk. *His* and *how are yous*. Everybody is getting ready to go to the gravesite. Finality is in the air. Someone hands me that crutch.

I'm not ready. How can they just switch? Change gears? Go from mourning my mom to socializing? Go back to their lives?

Don't they get it? She's gone. I'll never see my mommy again. She 'll never hug me or talk to me. But wait. She's just four steps away hidden under that shiny wooden box.

"Why did they close the casket?" I grab Robert's arm in a panic. "I need to see her again."

He takes that same funeral worker aside and minutes later, the four of us are standing over our mother. This time the fear is gone but not the panic. I cradle her hands in the only hand I can. That arm still refuses to move. It's so heavy, glued to my body, strapped against my chest, dead. Like Mom.

Her hands have been such a comfort all my life. I start to trace the squishy veins with my fingertip like I've done so many times over the years. I stop, confused. They're not warm or squishy anymore. Instead they are cold. Ice cold. I've never felt a body this cold. And flat. So flat, I barely see them. I kiss her forehead, but she's not there. She is not there. She doesn't even smell the same. This is not my mommy. I slide my hand out from under hers.

That's it? Goodbye? The end?

Frozen. Shocked by the incomplete finality. It can't end like this. I need to tell her so much.

I love you. See you later. Goodbye. Some sort of greeting to make parting bearable.

Or. *I need you. I'm so sorry. There's still so much you need to teach me. There are so many things we need to do together.*

How do I continue? How do I live? Nothing can make parting bearable.

5
Cut it Off

Lying on the couch with a hot towel soothing my whiplashed neck, Grami reads the Bible to me. I hear her, but not really. My thoughts are everywhere and nowhere at the same time. The funeral was only a day ago. I need Jesus the rescuer, ready to wade through pain, death and hell itself to find me, grasp my hand, and pull me safely through.

Grami, Aunt Jill, and Teressa try to comfort me, each in their own way. Mostly they are just there, not knowing what to say.

I exist in a concussed fog. Everything is muffled. The edges are blurred. The fog is encompassing, suffocating. I'm like helpless tumbleweed blown around by the fierceness of this world. This is death.

Grami's voice transports me back into my childhood.

·   ·   ·   ·   ·

Bounding down the stairs, at the landing, I peak around the corner.

Grami sits in her spot, a fancy and flowery loveseat with twisty arms, fingering through a three-ring binder. The thick, white binder is full of notebook paper and clear plastic sleeves. The pages are covered with hundreds and hundreds of prayer requests accumulated over the decades. Little scraps of paper, three by five cards, corners torn off paper bags, whatever she had at arm's length, hang out and fall out.

Pulling her glasses off her nose, they fall around her neck as she looks up at me. Another pair sits atop her silvery white head. The pair resting on her

Bible has one earpiece. Bibles of every shape, size, and version fill the bookshelf next to her. We've scoured hundreds of garage sales and little antique shops in search of these treasures.

I snuggle in next to her, burrowing my face into the folds of her shiny, red dressing gown. The warm comfort of her Bibles, three-ring binder, and half-dozen glasses envelop me. This is home.

She plucks a blank 3-by-5 card from a stack, lines up one of Grampi's old credit cards along the top line and writes my mommy's name, Janet Arlene. She slides the credit card down to add the little J loop. Lining up the credit card up with the second line, she writes Angela Dear. Adding a tiny g loop. The next three lines are for Teresa, Ursula and Micah. They don't have any little loops.

Micah runs in from the kitchen, handing me one of his Matchbox cars. He instantly takes it back and disappears behind the couch.

Summertime at Grami's. Mom gets a break and Grami showers us with the gospel. She has given me more Bibles then I can count and told me, "Jesus loves you more," until it's part of me.

We take evening walks around the small town of Morton, Illinois. Little shops, old and new, line Main Street. An antique store. A five-n-dime. Mom-n-Pop sandwich shop. And just past the courthouse, massive blocks of white limestone stacked high into the sky, the A&W Root Beer Stand. We get root beer floats with whipped cream and a cherry on top. Grami gets a small chocolate cone.

A few streets past the Apostolic Christian Church, we tend flowers planted at my great-grandparents' graves.

Oh, the adventures we have in Grampi's shed, transformed into a fort. Whiffle ball with the cousins goes into the night as Grampi turns on the back porch light and the air chills. I sniff back the snot before it runs into my mouth.

Days are spent playing house on the front porch. Grami watches from the porch swing. Grampi, perched in his chair, the only one with armrests at the head of the kitchen table, watches his beloved Chicago Cubs. The comfort of baseball echoes through the screen door.

．　　．　　．　　．　　．

Grami's voice, reading those familiar words, sucks me back to the present.

"How did Mom die?" Finally getting the courage to ask.

"Her neck broke." Grami quietly replies. "She died instantly." We just sit there, neither knowing what to say. Without a word, she gets up to go into the next room. A few seconds later returning with the *Rensselaer Republican*.

The local newspaper is dated January 24, 2001. The front-page article above the fold, *Woman dies in early morning car accident*. I read, "...pronounced dead at the scene... sustained blunt force trauma..." And then close to the end... "a witness reported... Angela... failed to stop..."

What? A witness? No. It was my fault? I killed my mother? I can't breathe or talk. I manage to choke out a few words through the sobs but Grami can't understand any of it. She's hard of hearing and could barely understand me even if I weren't crying and talking at the same time. I run out of the room to find the only other person in the house, Robert.

"Is it my fault?" I cry out to him.

"Has your memory returned?" His emotionless calm confuses and angers me.

I shake the paper in his face. Are you that oblivious? Not Grami, she sees what lies behind my sobs.

"God is in control of all this. He's the one who took her home and just used you."

Her words do not comfort.

"But did I run the stop sign?"

Waiting in the silent void, for any explanation.

What do I do with this information? How do I get beyond this? Do the dead forgive?

．　　．　　．　　．　　．

"Can I make you something to eat?" Jill's soft words follow me as I stumble up the stairs to hide in my room.

My mom's baby sister. Just twelve years older than me. I have wonderful and amazing memories of us growing up together that could fill the red leather-bound *World Book Encyclopedia* set of my childhood. I worshiped her and ate up all the attention she lavished upon me. I didn't care that most of that time was spent cleaning her already immaculate home. I was doing it with her.

"I'm not hungry." Frustrated, I forge on.

My life is gone. For good. Mom is gone. I will never use my arm again. I barely care. I live in a fog. I'm just surviving. I do what I'm told. I go where I'm taken. Food? I can't taste it so why eat?

No one understands the pain I'm in.

"It hurts." I yell down at her.

"Your arm?"

Really? Don't you get it? It's paralyzed. I have no idea if it hurts. I can't feel anything anywhere.

I am numb.

"I miss her so much."

Physical therapy was a joke. A joke. I'm completely helpless. I can't do anything for myself. I can't tie my shoes or put on my own bra. My hair has been in a French braid for a week. It's the only way to keep it nice without asking for help. And this helplessness was made abundantly clear in the last two hours.

.   .   .   .   .

The receptionist hands me a clipboard. I notice but don't care. She places it on my lap. I still don't move. Jill sits to my right, Carol on my left and Robert leans against a doorway across from us.

One of them picks it up and fills out the mountain of paperwork.

Two women come out.

"Hi Angela, I'm Sarah and I'll be your physical therapist. This is Kathy, and she'll be your occupational therapist."

"Hi." My meager voice floats away. Why do I have two therapists? And what's the difference? Oh, never mind, I don't care.

They take us back. We spend hours running through a battery of tests and exercises. But that arm doesn't move. This is all so pointless. It just hangs at my side, the dead weight pulling it from the socket. The circuit is broken. The muscles are no longer connected to my brain.

Kathy explains we are going to learn how to do things differently. We are going to figure out what I can do.

I don't care.

My left arm gives one thing. Pain. Real pain. Excruciating pain. Pain without end. Pain without solution.

Cut it off. Just cut it off.

I ache for her.

. . . . .

"Your stomach is growling." Jill persists.

I stop mid-step, wondering...

Really? Am I hungry? I didn't hear or feel the growl. All I can feel is the incessant, excruciating ache that fills my chest cavity.

Cut it out. Please just cut out my heart.

6
Force Vectors

"I'm ready to come back to school."

The dean of the school of Aeronautics & Astronautics is on the other end of the phone.

The world around me is clearer. The fog is lifted. I see again. And I'm sick of people making decisions for me. Get off the couch, Gala. Stop feeling sorry for yourself.

Choosing to live again, I strap my arm against my chest, and shove it out of my mind. Shoulders back, well the right one, anyway. Nose up, I shove that nagging ache deep inside.

I have a plan and this little bump will not stop me.

"Are you sure you should be coming back this semester?" His concern is valid. The accident was only two weeks ago.

Dead mom, dead arm and I want to return to one of the hardest programs at Purdue University, let alone any university, has to offer.

"I'm only three semesters from graduating." I plead with him. "I fought too hard to give up now."

·   ·   ·   ·   ·

Three years earlier, I run out to the mailbox. Barefoot, I barely feel the little rocks jabbing pink flesh. I get there just as the truck pulls away. It's finally here, but the envelope is too small to be good news. Tearing it open, the first words, "We regret to inform you," confirm my fears.

I run through the house to the backyard, where Mom stakes up one of our tomato plants.

"They said no." Handing her the letter.

Her dirt covered fingers take it from me. "Well, I guess you need to go talk to them. It's a standard form letter. They can't really see you through those basic questions on your application."

She's right. We don't give up. The next morning, I am in the admissions office, asking to talk to someone. Someone who can see what I see in myself.

The receptionist takes my rejection letter to a woman in the back. Together they disappear into another office. I imagine them trying to figure out what to do with me and my strange request. All I want is my rejection re-evaluated. Am I the first person to make such an appeal?

"Hi, my name is Judy. I'm one of the admissions counselors." Judy holds my letter, the other two ladies in tow. "Would you like to come back and talk?" She motions. Under her name on the door she's identified as the dean of admissions and a licensed counselor.

"I want to talk to someone about why my application was rejected." I sit opposite her.

She fingers through my file, and says, without looking up. "Your chemistry and calculus grades during your first year at Indiana University were not very good. You graduated with a fine arts degree, and we don't think you will succeed here in the school of engineering."

"That first semester at IU was very difficult." I explain. "Several things happened my senior year in high school, but if you look at my high school math and science scores..."

"We look at the most recent degree and scores," she interrupts. Her body straightens. She looks as if she's going to stand and finish with a polite thank you, ushering me out the door.

I need her to hear me, to see me. Acceptance to Purdue is the only possible outcome. What can I do to get her to stop? To listen? I shift to the edge of my chair, motioning as if to reach across, but stop and place my hands on the front edge of her desk.

"My dad was shot and killed in Brazil; my mom remarried; my grampi died; I changed my name to be accepted by my new step-father all during my last year in high school." I vomit out the words before she has a chance to dismiss me. I pull my shoulders back, grabbing the armrests and interlock my legs. "Then I graduated and went off to school expecting to double major in biology and chemistry."

Judy exhales settling back. Her hands rest in her lap. "I'm a licensed counselor and understand how life's circumstances can derail you." Her eyes meet mine, inviting me to open up.

"My dream is to become an astronaut. Purdue has graduated many astronauts and is only thirty minutes from home. It's the logical choice."

We spend several minutes discussing my life, and Judy seems genuinely interested in my future. She finally concedes. "We can look at a probationary admission into the school of science for a semester."

I leave the office with a different piece of paper in my hand and take it straight across the courtyard to sign up for engineering classes not science classes. Bursting with pride, I can't wait to get home and tell Mom.

· · · · ·

On a groggy Monday morning, I hear someone in the kitchen below. *Mommy!* My heart soars, as I roll over and push up. My body crashes down when that arm refuses to respond. It wrenches internally, slicing pain through my shoulder.

Oh yeah, no Mommy, no arm. Must be Grami.

I disintegrate into the mattress, locked away with what used to be my arm. The house is cold and dark, taking me back to that fateful morning two weeks ago. A weight overwhelms my soul. Jill sleeps in the bed next to me, Teressa on the futon under the window. The waterfall still trickles over rocks and ice.

Two weeks. Not much time to recover. I still need help with daily tasks. I don't have a car and can't drive anyway. My first day back at Purdue, and Grami will drop me off.

"Give me a few minutes, and I'll help you." Jill rolls over, as I'm trying to get dressed. She comes back from the bathroom with a brush. Obediently, I sit on the corner of the bed, frustrated I'm unable to do this on my own. I can't enjoy the love and attention being lavished upon me. She gently removes the braid and runs her fingers through my hair. Before I know it, the French braid has returned, and she is latching my bra. Stepping back, she allows me to finish.

Slipping my feet into Adidas running shoes, I walk down the hall to tie them. Kathy and I have been working on this all week in preparation for this morning. I'm finally getting back a small bit of independence. Without pulling the Velcro apart, I slip the strap over my head, and let my arm fall as I sit on the top stair.

I press my body against the railing to stabilize the shoulder. Grabbing my left hand, I place it on my shoe. The fingers deliberately, and too forcefully, clamp on to one string. My hand is not paralyzed, but it is numb. I don't have sensory feedback to know how hard to hold. Step one complete. No time to rest, my brain works hard to keep the fingers engaged.

I tighten the first knot, but the bow will take a little more work. I loop the string in my right hand, placing it on my shoe. Holding the left hand in my right, I grasp the loop as close to the shoe as possible. When I let go, the hand falls pulling the shoe string taut. With my right, I loop it and tighten. Success. Well sort of, it's a little loose but will do.

One down, one to go. Oh, I need to fine tune this process.

Eyes closed. One slow breath. I steel myself for the second shoe.

Teressa comes up behind me. She circles around, kneels, and simply, without a thought, ties my shoe. *It's too tight. Will you do it again? Never mind, I can't ask.*

"Thanks." Dying a little inside. The ache in my soul wants to rise, but I shove it back where it belongs. Hidden. Safe.

She smiles, but her eyes betray her grief... or is it pity?

We haven't left the house, and I've already exhausted my energy for the day. Things take so much longer now. We're already late, and I haven't figured out how I'm going to wear a winter coat with my arm tucked into a sling, not to mention carry my backpack and crutch all around campus.

Jill holds up my coat. I slide my right arm in, and she wraps the rest around me. I'm not very confident this is going to keep me warm or that the wind is not going to blow it off. Heaving my backpack up onto my right shoulder, I rest on the crutch as the bag slips to my hand.

I take one deep breath in exasperation. My head falls back against the doorframe.

"C'mon, Grami we need to go." I look to Jill, pleading. *Help. I can't be late.*

Expecting life to return to the pre-accident ease. *Maybe I just need a few more days.* I reason, still in denial.

"Here, Mom, I'll do that." Jill takes the little glass bowl, just like the one with oatmeal.

Clink.

.   .   .   .   .

The door is closed. Oh crap, the door is closed. I fold the sling back and look at my watch. Of course, it's closed. I'm late. Now what?

Panic creeps in, but I can't walk away. I pull the sling back over my hand, hike up my backpack and reach forward, turning the doorknob. Nothing is going to stop me. Nothing.

Creek! No sneaking in. Where's the WD-40? I find myself standing in the front of the room five steps from Professor Howell. She looks over but continues to lecture. The classroom is small, thirty students. Not just any thirty. These are my friends.

They are the biggest reason to return this semester. We've endured the last three years together. Taking all the same classes and spending every other semester at our CO-OP jobs all across the country. NASA Johnson, NASA Dryden, NASA Ames, Boeing, Rolls Royce and Lockheed Martin.

I ended my first semester at Purdue with a 4.0 GPA, a CO-OP position with NASA Dryden and one of the few coveted spots in the School of Aeronautics and Astronautics.

We can't do this program without each other. I can't do this without them. Now they're all staring at me. That all too familiar look in their eyes.

Looking down, I move my crutch forward. I can't delve into that pity.

John gets up and gathers his things, allowing me to sit at the desk right inside the door. I smile and softly thank him.

Okay, maybe I can just slide into this chair and disappear.

I lean my crutch against the wall.

Newton's equal and opposite show up with a crash. Yes, literally a crash. As I turn to sit, my bag brushes the crutch. True to Newton, it slides. In slow motion. Down. Down. Crashing down.

I just wanted to slip into this room, unseen. The laws of motion continue as the backpack slips off my shoulder, falling against the desk, nearly pushing it all the way across the aisle and into Julie. I manage to catch it, well to be more precise, it catches me. Jerking me into the chair, the bag falling between my feet.

Professor Howell stops talking. The air is sucked out of the room. No one moves. Everything's frozen as if Newton's laws transform into mere suggestions.

A joke. I need to tell a joke. Maybe something about my arm? Or force vectors? "Well, Professor Howell, we could analyze all the force vectors at work here."

Instead, all I can manage is "I'm sorry." But I barely hear myself. Did I say it out loud?

Relieved as the earth returns to its normal rotation. She's lecturing again.

Leaning over, I right my backpack, quickly pull out my notebook and pencil. Clicking twice, two millimeters of lead eject.

I date the top line and neatly draw in a satellite and a few force vectors. Ah. Exactly what I need. I fill my brain with momentum and acceleration and mass and time.

The rest fades away. My mom. My arm. My pain. The accident. It all melts deep into my soul.

Forty-five minutes of peace.

Page after page after page. Calculations fill the pages. Pencil lead clicks. My brain works and rests in the pages of the green-gridded, engineering notebook.

Doctor Howell finishes her lecture, packs up the cellophane overhead projector sheets, and I'm surrounded. No, I'm not ready. I'm too tired to face the eyes. The questions. And the help.

Like the force vectors acting on the satellite, my friends exert forces on my soul, requiring me to see what I've tried to bury.

Tim grabs my bag, and we head down the hall. We round the corner, gathering in the student lounge. They clear a spot for me at the closest table and accumulate all the homework from the last two weeks. Each course from its own bin. It's a hefty pile. It's going to take some time to catch up.

I welcome the work. This work. Right here. My brain can rest in the work.

7
Severed Signals

Here we go again.

I recline on the treatment table, disappearing inside. Stabilizing my shoulder with her left hand, Sarah lifts my dead arm.

The routine. Three days a week for two hours, I submit to the routine.

First Sarah stretches my shoulder. I like this part of the routine. I get to relax. Disappear. Nothing's expected of me. I don't have to fight, fight to survive, fight to live... for just a few minutes.

Then we fill the hour with several physical therapy exercises. These basically consist of Sarah moving my arm. I can't do anything. This thing is dead. Paralyzed. Completely immobile, dangling at my side. It yanks at my shoulder. It endlessly pulls at the muscles and tendons. The pain. Oh, I don't even know what to say about the pain.

Exercises. If that's what you want to call them. My brain is not moving anything. Sarah is doing all the work.

What are the goals here? Expectations? A sudden spark of life? That's not going to happen. When Israel Rogel slammed into my car, my body flew into the driver's side door, but my head remained. This action forced the nerves in my neck to yank out of the spinal cord. The C4, C5 and C6 nerves are no longer connected to the spine.

The cervical spinal nerve four (C4) is a spinal nerve of the cervical segment. It originates from the spinal column above the cervical vertebra four (C4).

Yeah, I know more than I ever wanted to learn about the cervical spine.

This is a critical nerve. It controls the thoracic diaphragm and has inspired a medical mnemonic: *Cut C4, breathe no more.* That's right, my diaphragm collapsed. I stopped breathing. Good thing it was only on the left side, and it was only partially avulsed. Or not. I'm supposed to think it's a good thing.

But that moment without breath, I want that moment back. Pure peace. Contentment. Rest. Without need. Oxygen was not required, nor gravity. Was that heaven? Forcefully pulled back. Dragged out of the car. Hands wrenched from my mother. Oxygen forced into my lungs.

Even now, breathing takes so much effort. I'm too tired to want to breathe. Physically, I'm able to breathe. Emotionally. Not so much.

The cervical spinal nerve six (C6) shares a common branch with C5. They innervate many muscles, ranging from the rotator cuff to the distal arm functions.

I've developed a whole new vocabulary.

Before reaching the muscles, these nerves branch and link many times. This allows other nerves to take over if one is damaged. Unfortunately, too many nerves...

Stop, Angela. You can't walk in the unfortunate. It's safer to immerse yourself in your newfound knowledge of the cervical spine and brachial plexus.

"Let's move over to the arm bike, Angela." Sarah interrupts my thoughts.

She lifts my arm and places my left hand on the handle, holding it in place. I rotate the bike with my right, taking the left for a ride. This is ridiculous. Not sure what good we're doing here.

The routine continues in the second hour as Kathy takes over. Kathy is an occupational therapist. Her goal helps me figure out ways to compensate. We work on everyday tasks. She's helping me get my independence back.

I still have use of my hand, so that's good. There's that word again. Good is not the word I would use.

It's confusing. How can I use my fingers and wrist while the rest of my arm is paralyzed? I have more to learn about the cervical spine and brachial plexus.

Today is knife and fork day. Yea. I can hardly contain my excitement. Gotta learn how to feed myself. Again.

I feel like a child, starting from scratch. But I can't even get my thumb up to my mouth. So, I'm more like a newborn. Is using a knife and fork really that important? Fingers are just fine. Well, my right ones.

Kathy hands me the utensils. I jab the fork into a piece of Styrofoam. It's supposed to simulate the food I'm supposed to want to eat. I imagine a dripping, juicy steak. Mashed potatoes soaking up the rich juice. I lift my left hand with my right and grip the fork. When I let go, it falls to the table, flipping the Styrofoam. Good thing that deep brown juice was just in my imagination.

Ugh, this is not working.

Closing my eyes, I exhale and disappear inside. Kathy slides her hands under my elbow and over my shoulder, lifting and stabilizing at the same time. My eyes remain closed. It's safer here.

"You can let go." Her voice pulls me back.

Opening my eyes, white knuckles wrap fingers around the fork like a bat. They don't easily release. I concentrate until it jerks open. The fork and Styrofoam flip off the table. No juice.

"Let's put on your wrist brace." Reaching around me to retrieve the brace, she skillfully wraps it around my wrist.

I shrink inside. I don't want the "help" of a brace. I can use my fingers and wrist but the signal from my brain is weak and slow.

"Maybe if I stand, gravity will help me stabilize it." I'm surprised by my participation in the process, but then again, I can rest in Newton.

"Sure. That's a good idea." Kathy retrieves the forked Styrofoam.

Standing, I press my arm against my chest.

Not supported in the sling, sharp shooting pain fires through my arm. Pain, my constant companion.

Lowering my left hand with my right hand to the table, I once again grip the fork, then release the right. The left hangs, just dangles, from my shoulder. To get this thing to stabilize, I need to gather every available muscle. My neck and jaw tighten. I contract the trapezius, the only working muscle in my shoulder, hiking it up to my ear. At the same time, I flex my pectoralis major, supraspinatus and serratus magnus, internally rotating the arm.

There you go, stabilized and less painful. I lock out my elbow with my triceps (it still works). How do the triceps work and not the biceps? Oh, never mind. It just does. The arm freezes in place. Holding my breath, I recruit every muscle in my body.

Now I need to cut into the Styrofoam. The steak disappears.

The tiny *force vector* applied at the far end of the *moment arm* pops everything out of balance, sliding the whole precarious contraption across the table, taking me with it.

The brachioradialis, bicep brachii and tricep brachii refuse to hold on, collapsing the elbow. The supraspinatus and trapezius give in, slapping my bicep against my face. Maybe if the infraspinatus and teres major came to the party, the shoulder might not have folded up on itself, but they're not even connected to my brain. The pectoralis major is all that's left, internally rotating everything. My chest crashes into the table. White knuckles still grip the fork, hanging over the far edge.

The treatment room goes silent. Therapists jump to attention. Everyone stares.

Maybe using a knife and fork with untrustworthy muscles isn't the safest choice. See, fingers are better. All babies start with finger food. Forget the steak. Honey Nut Cheerios for me.

"Oh, Angela, are you okay?" Kathy wraps her arms around me, lifting me off the table.

"Guess we should take it a little slower." I'm frazzled but manage a subdued chuckle. I drop the knife and push up against the table. The forked Styrofoam, still attached to my left hand, catches on the edge of the table and stops me halfway up.

Kathy slips her arm under my shoulder, lifting. "I think we're done for the day." With her other hand, she pries the forked Styrofoam from my clenched fingers.

I stare, amazed at her ability to so easily move her left arm. Does she realize how big and amazing that truly is?

It's only been a month, but my brain has already normalized disuse. It doesn't even try to do anything with my left anymore, well except at therapy when I force it to try. And try is all it does. This thing hanging from my shoulder.

And I try. I continue to try. I try to care. I want to care. But I'm too tired.

Like the severed nerves, blocking brain signals from reaching paralyzed muscles, my spirit is severed from my body.

Three days a week, I'm driven to and dropped off for my standing PT and OT appointments. I have no choice but to fight. Are there other options?

8
More Than a Witness

I can't do this. Really. I can't.

C'mon just go over there. It's why you came.

Last time, I didn't have a choice. Last time, it was winter, and I wasn't alone. Last time was the funeral.

I could call someone. But who? I pull up the antenna and flip it open. Scrolling through my contacts, searching for someone who will understand. Listen. Help me find the courage. Ah, maybe Andrea, right at the top of the list. Yeah, she's an amazing friend.

It rings once, twice, oh good, three times. I tried. She's not there. I pull it down to hang up, then... "Hi Ang, you okay?"

"I'm across the street from the cemetery, but I'm too scared to drive over."

Not sure what I expect from her. I just don't want to be alone. I don't want to be scared. I don't want to hurt so deeply.

I want someone to hurt with me. To listen. To show me love. To care. I need more than a witness. I need someone to walk through this with me.

"I think you should talk to Jason."

Your husband. Really, you don't want to talk to me? I called to talk to you, not your psychiatrist husband.

I don't say any of that.

Defeated. "Um, okay."

She's talking about when he'll get home. I give a few more okays, anxious to hang up.

I'm going to have to do this alone. Why would I expect anything different?

Gathering the required courage and strength. "Okay, goodbye." Relieved and ready, the real work belongs to me.

He's going to call me later. I'm not going to answer.

I go to my truck and retrieve my Bible. Is God going to give me what I need? Or will He disappoint as well?

Does it truly matter? I don't have a choice. I must cross the street to visit my mother's grave. I close the Bible without reading a single word (my eyes can't focus anyway), and pull up all the pain, all the disappointment, all the anger. I build a wall and do it.

I don't need anyone.

I softly, purposefully walk across the grass to my truck. Pulling open the door, I toss the Bible and slide up into the cab. Twisting around, I slam the door closed with my right hand.

I can do this. C'mon. Oh, I can't.

No. No. No. Don't fall back into fear. Here we go. Key in the ignition. Pull down into drive. Accelerate. Stop sign. Cross the road. Turn slightly left and a quick right. She's buried in the far right corner. Wind around. It's coming up.

Unable to stop, I drive by. It's getting smaller and farther away. Fear forces my foot onto the brake. Flinging me forward, the seat belt tightens. Frozen, I stare in the rear view mirror.

I'll just drive around the perimeter and try this again. Slowly. I read gravestones. Old and new. Some are familiar. Most are not.

Back at the road. Do I go back across the street and start over? Or just go home?

No. No. No. Closing my eyes, one slow deep breath.

A choice.

Winding back around, I slow as it approaches.

Just a marker. The stone isn't there yet. Her name and two dates.

The truck glides to a stop. My right hand strangles the steering wheel. Releasing my grip, I pull it up into park and turn off the engine. Resting my head forward, I reach down, unlocking the seat belt. It flings up but gets wrapped around my sling-encased, paralyzed left arm. A not so gentle reminder... I did this. She's here because of me. I wrench my eyes closed, trying to fight off the demons. They are relentless. I believe every word, every thought, every lie.

I am alone. I am exhausted. I am in pain.

I am to blame.

The fire in my chest wells, expands, engulfs. My shoulders slouch. I shake my head to dispel the fear and reach over, opening the door.

The soft cool spring breeze. Sweet scent of flowers and the deep "woo" of a dove softens the pain. Is that God? Did He show up? Is He more than a witness?

A dark rectangle rests in front of the marker. No grass yet. I slowly encircle. I'm not sure what I'm supposed to do. What is the point? She's not here. In anger, I step into the rectangle and jump up and down. But instantly regret it, run up to the marker and kneel. Grief, hope and anger sit together like old friends. Words without words pass freely between them.

"Mom, I need you."

9
Greyhound

Buried inside Newton's equations once again. Safe. Secure. I can succeed at this. My first make-up exam.

Like a thunderbolt, the phone jolts me away from the desk. Who could be calling at this time?

Reluctantly. "Hello."

"You need to send money, now!" Ursula's boyfriend yells. "I'm going to check in the morning. If there isn't a bus ticket waiting, I'll drown her in the swamp. You'll never see her again."

I push aside my papers and look up at the clock. I can't deal with this. I managed a routine to maintain some peace in my pain-racked life. This threatens to turn it all inside out and upside down.

"Are you crazy? It's eleven o'clock. Greyhound is closed." I try to reason with Moonshine.

Moonshine. My precious, baby sister is dating a nasty, old man who calls himself Moonshine, and I'm trying to reason with him. I don't even know this guy.

"Let me talk to Ursula."

Greyhound opens at eight but that's the same time as my exam. Do I take the exam or go to Greyhound?

My professors are making so many accommodations for me. How much more are they willing? Who do I choose? My sister or myself? My future or hers?

This has been a recurring theme in my life. Whose life gets the attention, mine or my siblings? And when I put the focus on my own, I pay for it.

·   ·   ·   ·   ·

"Mom, she's telling the truth. He's a wicked man. I don't doubt it for a second that he would do such a thing." I plead with my mother.

But none of us saw it.

I've just returned from two years in Albania. A trip I took against Mom's permission but justified in my mind because "I'm old enough to make my own decisions, and I went to spread the gospel of Jesus Christ."

The sweet, little girl that used to be my sister is replaced by a distant rebellious teenager. I spent my entire childhood loving and protecting her. Now... now we find out that Walter, Robert's father, abused her the last few years.

"Why would she lie about that?" Still trying to convince Mom.

But Ursula's been lying for years and generally making Mom's life miserable.

He calls her Molly. Is it just a cute name? But then I hear that he leaves dead moles for her at the front door. What a sick demented gift. Is he calling her Molly or Moley? Did we miss the signs? Did I miss the signs? Or did we ignore them not wanting to upset the status quo?

I know she's telling the truth, but I don't tell Mom how I know. I don't tell anyone. I tell myself I'm fine. But really, I'm angry. I'm angry Ursula wasn't protected. I blame myself for leaving. I blame myself for not speaking up years ago. It's my job to protect her and to protect Mom.

·   ·   ·   ·   ·

I bound down the stairs skipping every other step. Robert's lying on the couch watching HBO. The TV room takes up the entire basement with a huge color TV as its centerpiece. All we have is a 13-inch black and white from Grampi. It's so big it looks like a piece of furniture. Mom has her Christmas village displayed on top.

I'm across the room in two seconds flat and plop on top of him. Robert's been in our lives for almost a year now. He's practically family.

Christmas break in "the big house." Really, that is its name. The little house is down by the quarry. An old limestone quarry filled with water and stocked with fish. Robert's brother lives down there.

Teressa and I each get our own room. The two kids share one. Mine has a canopy bed with yellow and pink flowers. I feel like a princess.

He pulls me down into a tight embrace, my back on his chest. Oh, this is amazing. Does it mean I get to have a daddy? Exhaling, I let go completely.

What? Stop. His hand goes down my panties. What are you doing? No. Move, Angela move. His other arm, like a bar across my chest, halts my breath, my actual life.

I scrunch my eyes closed and disappear, soaring high above the clouds. Safe. Wind flows through my hair.

My body feels it, but I don't. I'm on fire deep inside. I don't understand these sensations. It's wrong. I know it's wrong. I need to run. Wait, stop. He pushes harder. Ooh, ouch. My body jumps against the pressure and pain.

I'm back above the clouds, flying.

He pulls his hand out, wiping it on my stomach. Without a word, he releases the bar against my chest. I pop up and bolt up the stairs.

At the top landing and through the mudroom, Mom's in the kitchen making dinner. I'm so confused and not sure what to do. I stand there for a few seconds. Watching. She's so happy. Urs runs over to me, Mic in tow.

"What does this one say?" She reaches up, pressing a present against my legs.

"That one's for Micah."

He grabs it from her, runs over to Mom and begs to open it.

"You have to wait two more days." Mom turns to get some butter out of the fridge.

They're all so happy. This is such an exciting adventure. We could be a big happy family. We could have a daddy. I can't mess that up.

I turn into the kitchen. "C'mon Mic let's go play in the snow."

· · · · ·

"She's not here." Moonshine's voice breaks the memories. "Did you hear me; I'm going to drown her. She will never be found." Moonshine's words sting. A thick suffocating fire wells up in my chest.

I believe him.

My racing heart makes it impossible to sleep. Thankfully, morning comes quickly.

I gather my notebooks. It's just me and Robert in that same quiet, dark house. We don't interact. Our lives just pass by very much untouched by each other. He lives downstairs. I get the upstairs, my prison.

Everyone else has returned to their lives.

Getting ready is still very difficult, but I have new ways of doing things. My shoes are already tied, and I slip into them. I wet my hand and smooth out the French braid. The crutch leans against the wall in the far corner, unused.

A few minutes before leaving, I warm up my truck. Mom always wanted a bright yellow pickup. Unable to find one, I settle for a black Chevy S-10.

I take the same country road. The ice and snow are gone. That same route through the cornfields, past the farms and pigs and cows, and that intersection. I pause, but only for a few seconds. Any longer, and I might feel. That would unravel all the work I've done. I close my eyes, shaking my head as if to push it out. Accelerating, I'm past it once more.

Before I know it, the first sign for Lafayette rushes by. I've got three more exits to choose from. One will take me downtown and to Greyhound. Another straight to Purdue.

I've prepared for both.

Professor Howell is waiting. She's come in early. I studied all night. I'm ready.

But my sister? Will Moonshine hurt her, kill her? How many more lives will I take? The directions are scribbled on a scrap piece of engineering paper, resting in the passenger seat.

Why do I have to make this choice? Where's my mommy? The wings of a dove. I want to fly away and be at rest. Closing my eyes, I shake my head and...

Choose Greyhound.

·　·　·　·　·

After three days of anxious anticipation, I wait at the truck stop just outside town five hundred feet from the interstate. Another bus pulls in, number 465 from Fort Lauderdale, Florida. That's it. The door opens, and the first person, a woman, steps down sideways, looking over her belly with each carefully placed step. Leaning heavy on the handrail, she's learned the hard way her steps cannot be trusted. A thin white Chicago Cubs t-shirt stretches way too tightly over her rolls and creases. Feet and ankles spill through her strappy sandals. Round nubs tipped in bright, red nail polish.

A young mother is next, wrangling three small children and a car seat. Her youngest trips, grasping at her purse. It spills out onto the dirt. A teenager follows closely behind. He wears tight blue jeans and cowboy boots. Placing his worn-out guitar case in the dirt, he steps around the boy and gathers up the purse contents. She thanks him. Turning to her son, she yanks him up by the arm.

The driver brings up the rear. His face is creased with age and fatigue. He opens the baggage compartments. I walk over to the door, stretching up in search of my sister. The seats are too tall, blocking my view. Stepping up, it's empty, but I go all the way to the back to verify. No one left.

The bags all are unloaded by the time I'm back outside. A box and a large black garbage bag sit in the dirt. Both are labeled, "Ursula Gutwein."

What happened? Oh, Ursi! Did you miss the bus? Did Moonshine drown you in the Florida swamp? What happened? Why would bags show up without her?

I frantically gather up her belongings and load them into my truck. The drive home takes only ten minutes, but I'm panicked before I get there. I rummage through my papers but can't find the number. It's probably not even her number or Moonshine's for that matter. They are nomads. Couch surfers.

Ah there it is. I tossed it into the garbage, not wanting to deal with Moonshine ever again. I dial the number.

"Yeah?" A groggy voice answers.

"Hi. This is Angela, Ursula's sister. Is she there?"

"Nah. I think they're stayin' with Kevin." His voice fades away. "Hey Donny, you seen Ursula?"

A muffled response.

"Yeah I think she's at Kevin's."

"I sent her a bus ticket the other day. Do you know why she didn't get on the bus?"

"Uh, no. I gotta go."

"Wait a minute. Do you have a number for Kevin?"

"Nah. He dudn't have one. I gotta go." Click.

A knot, a fire wells up in my chest. The handset falls out of my hand, thumping on the floor. What do I do? Where is she? How do I find her? Is she okay? Fear and panic overwhelm. I'm frozen. The room swirls. I reach out, bracing myself on the desk.

Then a switch. Anger takes over. I can't worry about her anymore. I have given up so much. It's my turn. She's an adult, and she's making her own choices. I let go of her. I'm done worrying about someone that is continually pushing me away. This is the life she wants. I let her have it.

Pause & Breathe

Scan your body.

Is there tension? Pain? Where? What does it feel like? Does it remind you of anything? What do you need?

Move. Breathe. Feel your feet on the ground. Look around the room.

When has your mind left your body to help you survive?

Have you had the opportunity to support a loved one using this survival mechanism?

This is where trauma takes us to the very limits of language, where we cross into the threshold of silence. This is where we feel trapped. When we need to be heard, but there are no words.

During trauma and its reliving, the language centers of the brain temporarily shut down.

That's okay. Trust it. This is the process, and it isn't easy. In fact, it's painful. Trauma hurts.

Can you sit and be? Just be.

Flying Lesson.
Sometimes it's okay to step outside your skin.

10
Survival

Robert lingers at the threshold for a few seconds. His arms dangle. Fingers loop around the neck of a beer bottle. Fear smolders with suffocating perseverance. He never comes up here. We live separate lives. I'm safe up here. This is my space. It's a prison but at least it's mine. The fire travels into my throat. My eyes glaze, holding my breath.

I see him but don't look up. We've forgotten how to talk to each other. If I ignore him, maybe he'll go away. He shifts his weight from one foot to the other but doesn't turn to leave. Reluctantly, I lift my eyes.

He steps into the room, and a massive weight sinks deep into my rib cage.

No, go away. Gasping one gulp of oxygen, I grab my left arm and pull it up against my chest.

My eyes follow his deliberate steps across the room. He sits on the bed as far away from me as possible and hesitates. He doesn't want to be here either, but it's clear there's a purpose to his visit.

Every muscle tenses. I want to run, but the futon sucks me in like quicksand. Raw fear. Why is this the first time I'm afraid of him? What does he want?

"What are your plans?" Robert pauses but quickly follows with the real question. "When are you moving out?"

I've spent my entire childhood orchestrating circumstances to never be alone with him. I refuse to allow him to hurt me again, and I certainly am not going to need his love.

Now here I am in my most dependent and vulnerable state since childhood.

With him. Alone. In the same house for five months. Five months. Has it honestly been five months?

I press pause on the VCR. *Survivor* season finale.

Last year, Mom and I were here together watching the first season. Me on the futon and her above me on the Papasan love seat. I can almost feel her now. Her legs rest against me as she drops her hand to brush the top of my head. Her presence gives me strength.

She loved both the adventure and social game of Survivor. Resting on the dresser just in front of Robert is the marine survival manual she purchased in preparation for her shot on the show.

"The semester is ending next week." My voice cracks as I force the words past a lump in the back of my throat. Oh crap, I do need his love. I will never tell him.

"I have my last co-op term at NASA this summer. I'll be moving back out to California in two weeks." He knows I work at NASA, but I need to remind him. I work hard to gain his respect which manifests in a healthy fear. I fold my leg underneath, sitting up slightly. The quicksand gradually releases. My confidence builds.

"Where... will you... be living... in the fall?" His words are slow and calculated. He wants his girlfriend to move in, and that can't happen while I'm living here.

Half-surprised, half-relieved by this conversation. It's a long time coming.

He's kicking me out. Betraying my mother. She persisted in this marriage to ensure I would be cared for. He already has a girlfriend, and it's only been five months. Does he miss her at all? Am I the only one hurting? Did he even love her?

Oh, Ang, put your big girl panties on. It's time to move on. Does it matter? You love her.

I chose to live here with Robert after Mom died, because I don't like change. I spent my entire childhood moving all over the country. I just want to stop, to settle down in one place, even if that place is filled with my mother's ghost and her abusive husband.

I want to leave. Not really.

"Micah's helping me look for an apartment close to campus." I tell him, not willing to face what I'm feeling.

Robert leaves the room.

I try to take a deep breath but can't get the air past that lump. I grab the end of the sling, yanking it off my arm. Completely sick of this thing hanging from my shoulder. It's dead, numb and on fire. Or is that my soul?

The sling flies across the room. My body folds over, burying my face in the futon.

Mommy, I need you.

More than that, I need normal back. I want my life back. My everyday routine. My mom. I need my mom.

The ache in my heart grows tentacles, invading my lungs, my stomach, my throat and up into my head. I can't breathe or swallow. *Mom fix it.* The pain in my head shoots a knife through my eyes forcing them closed.

No longer supported by the sling, my arm bangs into my lap, jerking it farther out of socket. I wince, cradling it.

Leaning back on the futon, I exhale a small amount of tension and place that thing I can't feel or use on a mountain of pillows. It's not a part of me anymore.

I press play and escape into the world of *Survivor*.

11
The Nassau Program

21 May 2001

Broken. I am broken.

Josephine and I approach the guard gate at Edwards Air Force Base. Soldiers, dressed in military fatigues, rifles at the ready, block the way. Every car is inspected, badges verified. Proper authorization is required prior to entry.

That arm rests, paralyzed, in my lap.

In front of us, the Ford Expedition is motioned to the side, and surrounded by soldiers.

This process is required to get to work. I've done it a thousand times. But I'm not the same person I was five months ago. Waving us through, they seem not to notice. I have all the authorization they require with a sticker on my windshield and a badge around my neck.

We continue down Rosamond Boulevard along Rogers Dry Lake bed. The last recorded rainfall was over a year ago and then not even a tenth of an inch, but the brine shrimp stench welcomes me home. The signage at Lilly Avenue, small, unassuming, blue writing on a white background is the first hint of this historic location. Red arrow pointing to the right.

High on a pedestal, a dart-shaped jet looms in the center of the road. The paved road curves to the right, passing the x-plane. X-plane. Experimental. That's what we do here. We experiment in the lab, in the aircraft hangar and in the air. But can I still do that? Everything takes so much more then I have.

Like a sentinel, the X-1E, the first airplane to break the sound barrier, foreboding in a sea of green rocks, guards the main building. The iconic logo centered above the entrance still excites my dreams. A sharp red swath through a star-speckled blue orb, the letters, N-A-S-A, etched right through the center.

Building 4800, the main building, is my home. My mind ventures past the front doors, down the hall to the operations engineers' office, adjacent to the pilots. I flash back to the hours spent racing, light-footed, around campus, excited at the many and varied responsibilities assigned to a young engineering student.

How can an astronaut function with one viable arm? I'm malfunctioning.

Light-footed no longer, the dream is fading.

I freeze. Looking down, my feet refuse to move. I see Josephine out of the corner of my eye. She's oblivious to my hesitation.

The first time I walked through those doors, my mother was right beside me.

31 August 1998

My heart jumps. Explodes. "Look!" I practically leap out of my seat; my whole core engages pulling me towards the steering wheel.

The sign is so tiny, normal. A small, white rectangle with blue writing announces our arrival at NASA.

"Wow. Holy cow, look. We're here." I drive around the pedestalled dart.

"You did it, Gala." Her smile, the sparkle in her eyes, reaches into my soul. "You're here."

My shoulders straighten. I am lifted by her pride. Indestructible, my smile matches her own. We park in front of the visitors' center and walk around four full-size aircraft on display. I've never seen planes like these. They have sharp lines. One of them has wings that sweep forward. They all proudly display the iconic NASA logo.

Ten months ago, denied admittance into Purdue's School of Aeronautics and Astronautics... now, welcomed into NASA... in four years, astronaut.

5 October 1998

Parked in front of building 4800, the X-1E casts a shadow on my Subaru Impreza. Foreboding no more, it's a friend, a partner in my dream. I make the final connections between the military hardened laptop and the GPS antenna mounted on the roof. Eddie, my co-worker and constant companion on these little adventures, completes the connections in his red pickup. It's hard to tell if the red is from the rust or the twenty-year-old enamel.

I fire up the GUI, that's graphical user interface to the unversed, to ensure the antennas are talking to each other. We drive around the green sea of rocks and loop through NASA Dryden Flight Research Center's buildings and hangars. Passing by hangar 4826, we park, side-by-side, at the end of the runway.

Final checks, hardware and software, complete, watches synced. I drive out onto the lakebed, past the DO NOT ENTER AUTHORIZED PERSONNEL ONLY sign, all the way to other end of the runway and turn around.

I'm authorized.

At the appointed time, the alarm chimes, and I accelerate. The computer screen comes alive. White numbers on a black background scroll up faster than I can read. We speed past each other skidding to a violent stop at opposing ends.

I mark the end of the first test with a simple keystroke as if that wasn't the most amazing thing I have ever done in my life.

20 December 1998

"This is my grand-daughter. She works on The Nassau Program." Grami introduces me to her pastor.

With a wry smile, I shake my head, turning to look at Mom. She smiles back, letting out a soft chuckle.

"No, Grami, I work for NASA."

I offer my hand.

"She's studying to be an astronaut." Grami continues as if not hearing me.

"I'm at Purdue studying Aeronautical and Astronautical Engineering." I correct again.

21 June 1999

I pop out of the golf cart in front of hangar 4826, pre-flight check procedures in hand. My GPS system is ready for its first flight test. The ground antenna is mounted atop building 4800 and wired to the computer in mission control.

Bouncing with excitement, I step through the open hangar door.

"Hey Tom, everything set?"

"Yep, we're good to go."

"Okay, we'll step through this on the radio," handing him the procedure.

I make a cursory walk around NASA-836, NASA's F-15B flight research aircraft. My GPS modem and antenna are affixed to the flight test fixture mounted to the centerline. I bend under the aircraft, grabbing the antenna. Satisfied, I bop out to the golf cart.

Next stop, building 4800 and mission control.

24 October 2000

I stand forty feet off runway 22 dressed in the iconic white over-suit ready... ready to recover the spacecraft. Wow, I can't believe this is happening.

Before it comes into view, two distinct claps, in quick succession, ring through the atmosphere. The sound wave penetrates Roger Dry Lake bed, sending a jolt up through my feet.

Just before two in the afternoon, a small white speck in the distance makes elongated S-shaped maneuvers. Growing bigger with every second, it's heading straight for me.

20:59:47 Coordinated Universal Time (UTC).

Space Shuttle Discovery touches down on runway 22 at Edwards Air Force Base. Right, smack dab, in front of me. Like a freight train, the orbiter zooms past. The sound is deafening even with two sets of ear protection, one custom molded to my ear canal, the other completely covering. Not to mention, it's been a glider since the final orbital insertion maneuver. The vehicle touches down at 221 miles per hour, back wheels first. The nose gently kisses the runway.

Space Transportation System-92 (STS-92) marks the 100th space shuttle mission.

Explosive bolts fire, ejecting the protective door and releasing the drag chute. The nose pops up momentarily and settles back down. It's halfway down the runway, and we are already at work. We document and measure everything left behind. We measure the width and distance made by the tires. We document an errant bolt 5 feet 2.7 inches from center.

We gather and diagram the drag chute location. We record landing and stopping distances. All the way down the runway, we perform our job.

I stand 25 feet 7.6 inches behind the space shuttle.

Mesmerized.

Entranced.

In disbelief.

The three menacing nozzles, each big enough to stand inside, caution my approach. Two others, smaller (I would have to kneel to fit.) flank the main propulsion engines. These are the aft orbital maneuvering system (OMS) engines. On the starboard delta wing, just above the elevons, *Discovery* still displays the original worm-like NASA logo.

For a few precious moments, I allow my childlike awe. One day. Oh, one day in the future, could it be? The dream, so close, I can taste it.

Dave McAllister, my mentor, walks up behind me. We smile at each other, a smile that says so much. The rare air we breathe in this once-in-a-lifetime, extraordinary, inconceivable moment. No matter the singularity of the moment, we still have a job to perform. He motions to the main landing gear. I nod, approach the left gear and document the tread depth. Dave performs the same task on the right.

We continue our inspections around the entire craft. We document scorched tiles, broken tiles and missing tiles.

Our inspection complete, the time has come for the crew to exit the orbiter. A tug maneuvers the Crew Transport Vehicle into position adjacent to the access hatch on *Discovery's* port side. After several minutes, it disconnects from *Discovery* and parks off to the side. I ascend the stairs, adrenaline flooding, entering through the open hatch.

18 May 2001

My cheeks fold up and eyes crease together. The muscles move to form a smile, creating the illusion of happiness.

"Click." The flash fires. My face relaxes back to neutral. Leaning against a pole, the street sign above my head reads, "Historic Route," like a banner on the top and bottom. The shield, sandwiched between reads, "Oklahoma U.S. 66."

Josephine and I swap places, and I capture her likeness under the same sign. My last trip out west, just the back roads this time. We've seen pueblos and plateaus, buffalo statues, buffalo grazing and buffalo burgers. We ate the burgers. A little dry and well done for my taste.

The forced, facial muscles form another smile, mimicking Josephine. This is fun, right?

Handing Josephine the camera, I gather up my dangling arm and stuff that hand into my jean pocket. The arm bounces uncontrolled from the shoulder. Bang, it yanks back. Bang, it yanks forward. Up. Down. Right. Left. With each step, it pulls at the muscles and tendons. I ignore the pain. Is it even in the socket anymore?

Two blocks down, at the corner of First and Main, a large white building comes into view, the old Coleman Theater, restored to its former glory.

In Miami, Oklahoma, pronounced my-am-uh, a name of Native American origin, Route 66 curves down A Street (one block west of Main) until Steve Owens Boulevard, where it returns to Main Street, but we can't miss The Coleman.

The vintage green sign crawls up the side of the building, COLEMAN in white. We round the corner, entering under the old marquee. I do enjoy history.

The expansive ballroom lobby decorated in extravagant beauty. Massive columns frame intricate murals along the walls. But it's too big, too much to take in. The details are lost to the eye, and lose their power to draw the soul into rest. My feet lose touch with the ground, as a twenty-foot chandelier pulls my eye upward. The extravagant absurdity continues on the ceiling. My senses cannot integrate the copious indulgence.

My eyes find natural light entering through double glass doors at the far end. A small green sign announces, *Celebrity Park*.

Through those doors is a serene little pocket with a fountain and benches. Picking a bench, my soul drinks in the sound of water, and the deep "coo" of a dove. Closing my eyes, the sun soaks through the eyelids, relaxing my forehead, face and jaw. A breath slowly escapes as the sun soaks down into my chest and lungs and gut. It heats and soothes, and softly allows my lungs to fill with life.

The ache in my heart swells with the fire of the sun, and my soul rests with the sounds of life.

Despair itself is hopeful if it is honest.

21 May 2001

The SR-71 looks jet-black, silhouetted against the marine blue horizon reaching as far as the eye can see, but is a dark blue to camouflage against the night sky and to increase the emission of internal heat. Resting in front of hangar 4826, the wing panels are relaxed, leaking fuel into pans strategically placed around its entire circumference.

It is not designed to be on the ground. It is meant to fly, and to fly fast. In that sweet spot, soaring through the stratosphere at Mach 3, the titanium alloy expands, sealing up.

My eyes follow the thin red pinstripe running down the fuselage, down across the tarmac, through the military hangars miles away, tripping over Joshua Trees and tumbleweed. Stumbling in the barren Mohave Desert, I am leaking. Grounded. Weighted down by gravity and grief.

I am not designed to be on the ground.

Leading Josephine through the open hangar door, like leading a guest through my home, down the hallway to the bedrooms. But it's different now. I'm different. I'm as useless as this useless arm stuffed in my jean's pocket, bouncing and banging against my torso. That blue orb painted and plastered on every building and aircraft fiercely becomes a barrier. The welcome I once felt is gone. My dream is fading.

The F-15B is still parked at the south end with its flight test fixture mounted to the centerline pylon. The north side is home to the X-43. Also referred to as the Hyper-X, the X-43 is NASA's unmanned scramjet hypersonic research aircraft. These aircraft are my friends. My partners. I've worked on their designs. They've clarified my dreams.

Wide-eyed, she snaps picture after picture. "Stand over here." Josephine directs me to the back of the Hyper-X.

Just over twelve feet long, it's tiny but packs a wallop with a top speed of over Mach 9. The ground-servicing cart, bigger than the actual vehicle, is my central task for the summer. I'm in the Research Directorate this term, working in the Propulsion Branch.

The Hyper-X vehicles are not reusable. There are three, each designed to go faster and higher than the previous. I stand next to the first, scheduled to fly after I leave. Since each vehicle will only fly once, the ground-servicing cart is one of the most important parts of the system. The vehicle must be working perfectly before we are cleared to launch.

My task this summer will be to design the cart.

We continue the tour through my home. I show Josephine the bedrooms, bathrooms, den and study. With each hangar, office and lab, I realize this is no longer my home. I smile. I brag. I allow her pride. But...

My dream, splattered all over that icy intersection thousands of miles away, gone in an instant I can't even remember. Blood, oil, fuel mix into something unrecognizable. Firemen mop it up, discarded with the hazardous material.

Wow, that's me. Discarded. Unrecognizable. Hazardous.

Pretty sure I don't care.

12
The Grief Bone

Adrift. Isolated. Deserted.

A sheet of stickers, on a clipboard, greets me. I fill out my name and arrival time and sit. I sit down in front of the opaque, sliding-glass window in a waiting room the size of a Volkswagen Beetle. I sit two chairs away from a woman in her twenties. Her clothes, skin-tight, show every roll of her three-hundred-pound body. Three boys, all under age four, scamper about. One crawls under my chair. Another trips over my leg. With an attitude of defeat, she reads *People Weekly*, "Who Will Survive?" on the cover. It's a few months old but I want to read about the Survivor II castaways.

My brain floods with memories. Hours upon hours spent with my mom. We were so invested in the lives of each castaway.

Mom, I need you. Please come sit with me. I can't do this alone.

I carry her weight, not on my back, but riveted to that dead pendulum suspended from my left shoulder.

That is the question... will I survive?

All my advocates are back in Indiana. I didn't realize... till this moment... how much they do for me. The door opens... "Mrs. Beaver?"

Mrs? They don't even take the time to know I'm not married. The ten-foot hallway is dark and lined with six closed doors, one at the far end and two on either side. I'm herded into the second on the right. The room is more like a stall. The exam table stops the door with just enough room to walk around.

She motions me inside, closing the door behind me. My chart thumps into the holder. I make a trip around the table, scanning the posters affixed with a tack in each corner. Nothing new here, same old pictures of the body, muscles and joints identified. *Sure, wish I had that* People *magazine.*

Minutes tick away as the anxiety rises. This is nothing like my physical therapy office in Indiana. This is a waste of my time and energy. I don't have anything to spare. Everything takes more than I have. To get here, I had to call for a new PT script, call to find an approved PT office and call to schedule an appointment. I had to fill out the mountain of paperwork, reliving the worst moment of my life over and over and over.

This is sapping my life, imperceptible, infinitesimal, invisible, requires an electron microscope to see.

It is not going to give me any relief or any use. It will not change anything.

. . . . .

The day is here... June 21, 2001... The Surgery. The surgery to give me back my arm. The surgery only three surgeons in the whole of the United States can accomplish. My surgeon taught the other two.

Doctor Kline's practice is in New Orleans. He went to school with my neurologist in Indianapolis, who personally asked Doctor Kline to take my case.

I sit alone, in front of gate thirty-two at LAX. I want my mommy. That limp limb dangling from my left shoulder continually prods, pokes and pricks at my guilt. At what I've lost. At what I've taken from my family. They don't have a mother, daughter, sister, grandma, friend because of me.

Now, I do this without her. I only have strength to do the next thing in front of me. My heart will have to wait. I wait for the gate to open. For the peanuts and pop. For the take-off and landing. For my grandmothers. And for the surgery to give me life.

. . . . .

"I can return nerve function to your arm, but it will take five years before you see any movement." Doctor Kline pauses to let it sink in. His kind eyes reach into my soul.

I start to speak but the knot, which instantly formed in the last few seconds (Where did that come from? We're supposed to keep my heart out of this.), stops all words. Instead, tears of boiling acid well up and roll out no matter how hard I try to fight it. Blinded behind burning eyes.

Reality sinks in. The fire in my chest shoots up into my head. I can't focus. I'm punched in the gut, directly on the grief bone. There must be such a bone. Like the funny bone, just as jarring, but deep in the gut.

My piercing cries, no one can hear, deafen me. I am dreadfully alone in room full of doctors and interns and... Robert. I wanted him here, but not just him.

·   ·   ·   ·   ·

"You're coming to New Orleans, right?" I look at Robert.

Josephine and I stand in the driveway behind Mom's van, all packed up, gassed up and psyched up. I'm leaving her (my mother) behind. I trust she will be safe in this house for the summer. I can't take her with me. I need to do this on my own. And I need something to anchor to... she is my home-base.

"You want me to come?"

Are you kidding me? What kind of question is that? Of course, I do, you are... how do I finish that sentence. Who are you? You have never been my dad, but...

Why do I still need this man in my life? He abused my mother and me. He rejected my sisters and perverted my brother's image of a man.

But he is the only father I know. He nurtured my brain, giving me a love of science and math. We spent countless hours on the driving range, giving me a persistent pluck.

"Yes, of course. I need you."

What I really need is my mom, exhaling... I guess he's the next best thing... that stings. It can't be true. Running upstairs, I call Grami. If anyone is the next best thing, it's my grandmothers. My next call is to Grandma Gutwein. They both agree to be there for me.

·   ·   ·   ·   ·

Robert stands with the interns. Trying to look clever, he asks a question about the supraspinatus... blah, blah, blah. I think he just made up that word. He smells of old sweat and stale beer from a late night on Bourbon Street. I don't have much hope that he'll explain any of this afterward, and he forced Grami and Grandma to stay behind.

"It will take a few more years before you will get any purposeful use. Nerves grow about a millimeter a day and the neurons in your brain have to rewire themselves." He explains handing me a box of Kleenex and turns his attention to his army of interns. "I will connect the nerves that innervate her neck and scapula to her bicep and deltoid..."

The explanation gets very technical. I turn inward.

I can't use my arm. At all. It is paralyzed. This isn't something that's just going to get better.

Big-eyed interns ask question after question, jotting down every word. An atmosphere of excitement fills the room. A case like mine doesn't come along very often.

I am dying inside.

Drawing pictures of my brachial plexus, he details which nerves he will "borrow from Peter to pay Paul."

I like that phrase. Paul and Peter have the same mission, but they focus on two completely different people groups. My nerves will have the same mission but will focus on to two very different parts of my body. How is my brain going to figure that out? Oh wait, I think Doctor Kline just explained.

I missed it. He says something about repetition and lots of therapy.

He and this surgery is my only hope to ever use my arm again.

The pencil slides along the yellow notepad. My mind gets lost in the scratch of lead along smooth, yellow paper. The storm in my brain calms. I'm beginning to hear his words and hope grows. The pictures help. I learn new vocabulary and the technical talk engages another part of my brain. I'm more comfortable here... in my brain, learning. I disassociate from my emotions and...

"You will need to continue your therapy three days a week. After about five years, your muscles will start to fire."

Doctor Kline just said that I will be able to use my arm again. Hope inches its way up, invading my brain, pushing out all that new vocabulary. Wait... five years? Really, it's not going to move for five years? The storm coils up, eddies build and boil over. Acid tears scald my cheeks.

The firehose drenches, suffocating me. I'm unable to speak. He continues.

"But they will be very weak. You will need to persevere many more years."

Persevere. The magic word. He wants me to pretend this is normal and... persevere. With force, I swipe my eyes dry. The tears and a little bit more of me are thrown across the room like they never existed.

Okay. I can do this. This will not beat me.

He talks of nerves and neurons and scars all the way up my neck. He performs more tests with a safety pin and a little hammer. This is good; I like tests. I'm good at tests. But the safety pin test, I fail. My arm is disinterested, refusing to participate.

Wait a minute... Scars?

What will it look like? Where did you say? I can't even form the question in my brain. Another wave swoops in, spinning me under the whitecap.

He continues.

"This is a long, slow process. Nerves are very sensitive. The pain will be intense. You will want to quit."

Nah, it won't be that bad, dismissing reality. Survival requires a little naivete. White knuckles swallow up the damp tissue. Softening my grip, I toss it across the room. Nope, I don't quit. It bounces into the trash but more importantly it lightens the mood.

"Do you have any questions?"

The tsunami of new words, fear, hope and pluck floods my brain. Pleading eyes look over to Robert. I'm unable to organize any of it into a coherent sentence. Robert offers nothing.

"Uh, sounds like you've got all the bases covered. Let's do this." Trying to sound strong.

Ripping off the top page, Doctor Kline hands me the yellow sheet with what will become of my brachial plexus... never to be the same again.

The interns joke about who's smarter: the rocket scientist or the brain surgeon. I manage to crack a smile, but I feel it... deep in my soul. Can I do this?

Endure or quit?

Doctor Kline transfers me to Ochsner Medical Center, located on the Mississippi River in Jefferson, Louisiana.

. . . . .

The atrium is open, airy, bright. Full grown trees reach high but don't even come close to the glass-domed ceiling spanning one hundred feet across and all the way down the entire concourse.

This is designed to put me at ease. It's not working; I'm busting at the seams.

After a morning full of poking and prodding, arms bandaged and bruised, I slump down into a couch adjacent to one of the water features scattered throughout the Ochsner Medical Center facility.

The water trickles down the multi-level waterfall... still not working.

A large hallway curves off to the right, an arrow pointing to the chapel. Find my comfort in Jesus? Where are you?

. . . . .

Just days after the surgery, I'm back in Lancaster, California.

My entire neck, all the way from my ear to my armpit, covered in a thick, white bandage. My arm still motionless, useless and helpless.

Or is that me... motionless, useless and helpless. Paralyzed. Petrified. Without purpose.

Adrift.

I finger through the yellow pages. *Hair Salons*. Oh, I don't care; I'll just call the first one, *Allie's Beauty Salon*. Remember, you're not going to let this beat you?

"Hi, uhm, I have a weird question. I just had major surgery, my arm is paralyzed, and I can't wash or do my hair." Reliving that moment all over again.

What does she think? Is she going to laugh? Please don't make me explain. I barely pause long enough to breathe.

"So, what I need is someone to wash and French braid my hair, without getting my surgical site wet, once a week for the rest of the summer. Is that something you could help me with?"

"Oh, honey. I'm so sorry. When would you like to come in?"

Relieved, she doesn't ask more questions. I set up the appointment and move on to the next phone call... finding a doctor for post-op care.

. . . . .

She gently removes the tape, peeling away the bandage. What does it look like? I study her face. She doesn't even blink, giving me nothing. I catch her eye.

"So?"

"You haven't seen it?" Her expression still stoic.

"No, is it bad?" I plead. "Doctor Kline said that is was going to be. Well I'm sure he didn't use those words. I need to know."

"Let me get a mirror." She moves to the counter, retrieving it.

I take it from her, slowing lifting. It's in front of me. I look, without seeing, all the way through the mirror to the opposite wall. A poster, half skeleton, half muscles. Major bones, ligaments, muscles and tendons labeled. She watches as my focus returns to the mirror.

I blink. Inhale. Close my eyes.

"I don't want to look."

Her hand closes over mine. "It's okay, maybe next time." She rolls my fingers loose.

Panic swells in. My grip tightens, yanking it from her. Hugging the mirror against my chest.

"No, I need to know. I can do this. Just give me a minute."

Eyes tight. Forehead furrowed. It's in front of me. Exhale. Slowly. Eyes open.

13
Rough and Rugged

I see it. Technically, my brain sees it. The shape forms at the back of my eye, inverted, as neurons in my brain transcribe it right side up. But the image remains hidden from me in the folds of my brain.

I place my finger on the small pea-sized bump an inch below my earlobe. It rolls away, sending sharp pain up through my ear. Thankfully, my hand obscures the rest.

. . . . .

A week later, sitting on the same exam table, holding the same mirror.

I slide my fingertip over the pea. It rolls. The pain lacerates into my ear. My brain releases more of the image.

The wound narrows to a thin red line until it reaches the clavicle, where skin pulls and stretches...

I squeeze my eyes closed, pressing my hand flat against the scar. The choppy, potholed trail meanders down my middle finger and across the palm, extending out either side, too big to be covered.

Squeezing eyes tighter, I press deep against the wound. My face explodes with fire, ringing out my ears. Determination forces a deep exhale.

I will not fall.

. . . . .

A month later, and this time the bandage will be removed. The fibers have closed over the open wound. The scar is complete.

Tape pulls away. The white, gauze squares fold down. More tape. It's off. Open. Ready to face the world.

I see it. I isolate the image in the folds of my brain. It is intriguing. The colors and folds and knots pattern an intricate trail across the landscape of my body.

It begins less than an inch below my earlobe. The skin is white, stretched over a small pea. Narrowing to a thin red line until it reaches the clavicle, where skin pulls over another larger pea, more the size of a marble. Here, like spider legs, the scar spreads up and around my clavicle. One dark purple leg inches its tentacle back up towards the ear. The rest of the scar makes the arduous trek up and over the marble, continuing its path to the armpit, where it hides just behind the tendon.

I slowly trace the rough and rugged track with my fingertip. Each bump, each marble, each pea, sends sharp, lancing pain deep into my gut. I wasn't given a choice. Doctor Kline barely mentioned it, barely asked me, said, it's this or permanent paralysis.

I feel it. Deep in my gut, I feel it. The scar sneers back, mocking me. *You deserve this. This is your punishment. You killed your mother.*

A permanent reminder of all that I did.

Closing my eyes, I try to breathe, but the gulp gets stuck and forms a knot. Heat builds in my face as I fail to get any oxygen. Lost. Lost inside my head.

Soft fingers touch my arm. "Breathe, honey, just breathe." The faraway voice, like a beacon, leads me back. My reluctant breath is too shallow. It's so much safer to stay lost.

"Good, again." The nurse squeezes my arm, pulling me closer to the surface.

The second fills my lungs. Heat dissipates from my face as my eyes open. The harsh world rushes in. No hiding behind a thick white bandage.

·　·　·　·　·

Angela Kari Gutwein　79

Now just an angry, red scar. Painful to the touch. Painful to my soul. A constant reminder. Not like I needed another one. This useless arm dangling from my shoulder is reminder enough.

I choose my standard NASA work uniform, jeans and polo shirt. My hair is still pulled back in a French braid. The rutted, red trail a stark contrast to my creamy, pale neck.

Exposed. Fully exposed.

The sling already brought the constant questions, "What happened to your arm?" Their smiles expecting a fun story. Falling out of a tree. A bike crash. A soccer injury. No one's ready for the real reason, including me. It just brings silence.

Now the rugged, red road slicing down my neck hints at something more. A knife attack? A mauling? I'm so broken, I can't even make up a fun story of saving some hapless child from an escaped jaguar.

Awkward glances are forcefully diverted up to my eyes or to the ground. Cover it? No way. I will own it.

Or does it own me?

After all, I deserve worse.

14
Not Alone

I walk across the street and into the student union through an obscure side door. A huge crowd is gathered, requiring me to squeeze in. It's eerily quiet. Several groups whisper to each other. All eyes are transfixed on the television. I start to push through but slow down as I begin to understand.

"... terrorists..."

I weave around three large pillars in the center of the room. Today is the job fair. I have several interviews scheduled. I can't deal with this today. Maybe in a few years, I'll have the strength.

"... airplanes..."

I continue through the arched doorway into the next room. Another TV. Another crowd. This is big, huge. But what is it? What happened?

I'm curious but focused. I need to stick to my plan for the day. My interviews begin in thirty minutes. Usually if I just stick to the plan, I don't get overwhelmed. The mass engulfs, halting my progress.

"Hey, what's going on?" I catch the eye of one. Her pinpoint pupils send chills through me. I know that fear. I've fought to bury it.

"They... um hijackers..." She struggles to find the words.

Looking past her, I see a passenger jet slam into a high-rise building. A fireball bursts out the other side. Is this real? It feels like the latest disaster movie. The banner at the bottom of the screen reads, *Terrorists hijack 3 passenger jets*. With plenty of time, I allow my gaze to linger on the TV for a few minutes. The footage replays the scene, switching between the two, burning it into my brain. The trauma, the assault is complete. It begins deep in my gut. The ground rises, my legs disappear underneath me.

Two towers. Two jets. Two fireballs.

The third aimed at our nation's capital.

The replays are interrupted. Breaking news, another jet is missing. A swamping fire in my gut threatens to unravel my precarious balance, but I've developed a very valuable skill these last nine months. Nine months? It feels more like nine years or nine minutes. Survival. Drench the fire to survive.

I close off. Shut down. Straighten out the stack of resumes in my hand. Amplify my focus. Zero in on what needs to be done in this moment.

Interviews.

Severing my gaze, I elbow through the throng. Ah, the hallway. Free. Wide, empty hallway. The crowd. The fear. The whispers. The newscaster. All behind me.

I clamp my eyes closed and freeze in place. The fluorescent lights shine through my eyelids, soothing the flaming tsunami. I breathe. One long deep breath. And another. The news feed fades until all I hear is my own heartbeat.

My eyes slowly open. The stack of resumes mangled in my clenched hand. I rush into an adjacent office, straightening the papers on an empty table. More deep breaths. I fold my sling back to reveal my watch. Fifteen minutes to get across campus.

I straighten out my sling, pulling the strap down around my shoulder. It hurts so much up around my neck. Nope, we can't focus on that. Ignore the pain. Bury the fear. Get the job done.

Strapping on the blinders, I'm out the door, down the hall and across campus just in time for the first interview. Completely shocked to find the whole world has stopped. Interviews are canceled. Don't they know how to keep going? Survive?

All dressed up with nowhere to go, forcing me to stop. No. I can't. Please don't make me open the wounds. I must remain strong. The only way to survive is to lock it down. Everything must remain buried. Feelings are the enemy.

I slump into a nearby chair, entranced by a crack on the far wall... transported deep inside. I refuse to look at anyone. I'll see it. I'll feel it. I'll know it.

I will fall apart.

Little groups gather. The whispers are back. I gradually start to see them as they gather around me. They comfort each other. And then it happens... I get what I've been wanting since the accident.

I am no longer alone. The entire country bleeds. Lacerated through the soul.

At least now, maybe someone will understand what it feels like to hurt so deeply that you don't even want to breathe.

Pause & Breathe

Scan your body.

Where are you holding? Can you release?

Trauma and pain and grief are messy and awkward and dirty.

You cannot heal without getting dirt under your fingernails. The real work is done in the dark. Deep under the soil, where we die and are reborn into unexpected, extravagant beauty.

But before the rebirth can happen, we need to willingly see it and walk through it.

Can we allow the hurt? No expectations. No needs. No shoulds and shouldn'ts.

To love another, we must let go of our ego and need. Can we sit in the darkness? Are we willing to be with our pain to see the suffering of another? If we take this journey together, we can be heard.

Don't try to fix it. Just rest here.

Flying Lesson.
Be willing to walk through hell.

15
Party Time

The dead-end street is lined with cars. I drive past them all and turn into the driveway. One spot left, right behind Mom's van. It's still there, sitting right where she left it. That familiar companion blasts through my chest, knotting up my gut.

Stepping out of my car, I zip my coat up to my chin to protect against the crisp night air, cocooning my arm against my stomach.

Off to the left, behind the four gooseberry bushes, one for each us kids, like we had at our old house in Francesville, the yard makes a sharp descent into the Iroquois River.

So quiet and peaceful. I love it down there. Tempting.

Off to the right, the driveway turns up to the house. Steam and ambient landscape lighting coalesce with the muffled voices, rising through the splashing, ten-foot waterfall and crashing into the swimming pool.

September 26, 2001. My birthday. Robert is throwing a party.

For me.

Almost too overwhelming to believe. Hope expands in my heart. Then a weight tightens like a noose as I slide up the latch, carefully pushing open the heavy, iron gate. Oh, please don't squeak. I can still run. Do I trust in this hope? Will I be loved? Or crushed? Which Robert is going to show up tonight? Almost on tiptoe, I want to be invisible. I need to be invisible. What do I do with this ambivalence? The tsunami overwhelms me, giving one choice.

To step up into the backyard.

To move forward. I'm the guest of honor. I've lost my invisibility powers. Loud noises. People. Crowds. So many things bother me these days. I don't understand. I can't remember when it started. Feels so normal now, though.

Run. You can still run.

"Ang." Josephine jumps up, wine glass high in the air. In her left hand. How does she do that? Does she even realize?

Praises erupt, and I'm stuck. Running is no longer an option.

"Happy Birthday."

"The party has arrived."

Melodious voices surround me offering the promise of a sweet evening. But my hypothalamus disrupts the normal flow. Instead of harmony, I hear only discordance in a cacophony of genuine wishes.

This is Robert's party. These are Robert's friends and family. But they were Mom's friends too, right?

Then hugs. Lots of hugs. I can't help but melt as each one brings me deeper into the moment. Escape is impossible but not desired. I need to get out here. No, I want to be here. My body is so confused.

"What are you drinking?" David wraps his arm tightly around my shoulder, leading me to the table. Wine. Champagne. Beer. Meat and cheese platter. Shrimp ring. Pretzels. Chips. And presents.

Lots of presents. Wild colorful presents.

I motion, too dazed to find words, to a bottle of merlot. My eyes can't focus. Too many voices moving in all different directions. David, still holding me tight, pours me a glass.

The back door swings open. Robert flies through carrying an exquisite chocolate cake perched atop a pedestaled silver platter. The pride of a chef serving his masterpiece to an acclaimed food critic.

Twenty-nine candles flicker in the breeze. The song instantly ignites, carried high into the night. The fight continues in my hypothalamus. *You can't run but you can disappear inside your head. Or let go and join in.* The lighthearted revelry makes the dangerous choice seem safe.

I let go, kenneling the guard dogs for the night.

Hours of drinking. Cake in crumbles. Wrapping paper lying about, crushed underfoot.

"I need to gather up some winter clothes from upstairs." I announce and disappear inside.

Up in my old room, I look out the window. The party, still going strong, is muffled by the window panes. It feels safer, less threatening, up here.

Observing from afar. It only takes a few minutes to gather the necessities. I shove a few sweaters in my sling and load up the right arm, resting my snow boots on top.

A smile escapes. I feel loved. I break through the caution tape and practically skip to the top of the landing.

Robert stands at the bottom of the stairs, like a guard. My brain wants to erect some protection. *Relax. It'll be fine.*

"What are you taking of hers?"

I hear it but can't process it.

Of hers?

I dismiss his accusatory tone. He's been so nice tonight. Why would I take anything that belongs to my mother? She might need it. In my mind, she's still here.

"I just need my boots and some sweaters." I smile. "I could use some help carrying these to my truck, if you don't mind."

Taking the first step, I lose control. The boots wobble atop their precarious perch and topple down the stairs.

"Ooh, see. I don't have enough arms." I chuckle to myself, smiling at him.

His arm moves to the railing, blocking the exit. My brain becomes more forceful. *Careful. It's coming.* He lifts one foot to the first step. My brain blasts another warning. *We need to put up a wall, at least.*

So many signs, signals and sirens. Ignored and dismissed. It happens in a flash.

"Let me see what else you have." The accusation, carried with the darts coming from his eyes, flies up the staircase.

There it is. He's back. With seven words, he destroys the entire evening.

Caution tape cut. Guard dogs fast asleep. There's nothing left to stop the arrows. The weight instantly rests heavy in my rib cage. Fire rushes to my face. Tears gather just behind my eyes. Fighting to gain strength, I force my foot to the next step.

With each step, anger grows and with it strength. Four steps down. I kick the first boot to the bottom. It settles behind him. I reach the second boot two steps later. Another stronger kick. This one bounces against the wall, ricochets off his leg and settles against the front door. At the bottom, I push around Robert, kick the first boot and bend over for the second. No longer assisted by gravity, my sling-encased, left arm dangles away from my body, releasing the sweaters.

I step over them, continuing through the living room, kitchen and garage, straight out to my truck. *This man will not crush you. Nothing's going to stop you.* Not even the trail of clothes, like bread crumbs, I leave in my wake.

Now what? Opening the door is impossible with my only useful hand full. Bracing the few remaining items against the door, I pull up to the handle. It's open but my clothes tumble to the ground, that one boot rolls under the truck and the door slams shut.

Oh, you've got to be kidding. I can't do this. Closing my eyes, I slouch forward, resting my forehead on cold glass. *At least my arm is free, now.* Shutting everything out, I search deep inside for something. Something to push me forward.

"Angela, you have a choice."

What, what choice?

"Will you live, or will you die?"

All I can do is survive, but I want to die.

"Okay girl, survive. Open that door. Gather your stuff. Take your time. Make as many trips as you need."

But I'm so tired. Please let me give up.

"Only carry what you can."

Back in my truck, everything gathered, ready to go. But I can't. Not yet. I need to thank everyone and my gifts. I need to load up my gifts. It's not their fault Robert's a jackass. *C'mon Ang, survive. Your only job is to survive.*

I make that same trip through the iron gate, past the waterfall and around the swimming pool. This time, silence is louder than the cacophony. Do they know? Did they hear us?

"Hey guys, thank you so much. This was amazing." I manage to smile through my burning eyes. It's too dark for them to see the dried tears. "Gotta go home now. I have class in the morning." Do they know the real reason? They seem to.

Nobody mentions the purple elephant standing in the middle of the table. Robert's still inside. The hugs are softer like I might break if they squeeze too hard. I don't melt into them this time. This time I must be strong. Feelings are weak.

Slumping into the front seat, the cold cab wraps around my weary, broken soul.

Escape. Run away. Freedom.

This is freedom?

The guard dogs are back at their post. They're not going to let me do that again. I'm thankful for my constant companions but this prison intertwines with every fiber of my being. There is no difference. There is no beginning. There is no end. I am the prison.

16
Moving Day

John, the mover, reaches up and grabs the rope. With a heave, the door slides down slamming shut. He locks it down, securing all I've accumulated in my cozy studio apartment these last eight months. But that's not all my things.

I lean heavily against the brick facade as they climb into the cab and pull away. They have directions to the next stop. I breathe in, realizing my last breath was almost a minute ago. With a clenched jaw, I tighten my core, shifting my weight away from the wall and onto my feet. If I don't hurry, they'll beat me there.

It only takes thirty seconds to make one last trip through the apartment. Entryway and galley kitchen occupy the same space. Cabinets and drawers stand open, empty. Bathroom, plain white, turns to thick mud as I slap out the light. The single room. Bedroom, living and dining room. Now just four eggshell walls with brownish-white carpet connecting them.

Good-bye.

With one last look, lights off, door locked, I climb into my truck.

Grami and Micah are already there. I can't do this alone, but I couldn't ask just anyone. Robert won't allow just anyone in his house. He intimidates. He pressures. He is prickly. My plan is to take everything that belongs to Mom and to me, put it on the moving truck and ship it down to Texas.

Texas.

I chose a job at Lockheed Martin, not NASA, working on aircraft, not spacecraft, because I didn't want to live in California's Mohave Desert. I love my job at NASA Dryden Flight Research Center but hate living in a desert. The sun bakes with nothing to block it. No trees. No clouds. Just hot dry air sucking every drop of fluid from every cell in my body.

After four days of interviews at NASA Johnson Space Center, the bureaucracy that is civil service halts any possible job offer. The dream officially dissipates. So, I settle.

This accident forces me to settle. My arm is strapped against my chest, useless. Everything requires more than I have. Nothing is easy. I graduate. I have a great job. But I'm barely surviving.

I'm so angry at... who knows... God... myself... my mother? My life is turned upside down and inside out. My plans crushed, wadded up and tossed away.

On autopilot, my car turns down the back road towards home – well, Robert's house. I don't have a home anymore. Soon all my earthly belongings will be packed up, loaded into a semi-truck and on their way to a place I've never been. Alone.

Two things wait for me – a job and an apartment. Neither of which give any promise of joy or fulfillment. The apartment looks like a lonely white box. The job, well that's not what I've been working towards these last four years.

But I'm still expected to be strong. To strap on my arm and charge forward. Did you hear it? The anger? I'm expected to be thankful for this lonely white box and exciting new opportunity. I am, yet honestly, no. Thankful for settling? What about my dream?

The intersection approaches. The. Intersection. The intersection that crushed my soul inside my crumbled Subaru Impreza Outback Sport.

I want to slam on the brakes and make a u-turn. Instead I sit up straight. My forehead furrows, eyes refusing to blink. Vigilant focus. It's okay. You'll be okay. All that's required of you is to hold your breath, hide behind the guard dogs and drive through.

Good job. Let's keep those dogs on alert. We have a lot to power through today.

I turn down South Iliff Drive and park in my same spot right behind Mom's van. Before I get out, the phone rings, and the truck pulls in front. My heart jumps, sweeping my gut under the waves, forcing a gulp of oxygen into my lungs and stomach. The storm in my brain paralyzes me. It rings again. John jumps out, waving. I force a smile. My brain can't figure out how to raise my hand. He smiles back and walks to the rear of the semi.

Oh, good, he's okay for now. Another ring. It's my cousin James. He needs to drop off the washer and dryer I bought from him. This will not go well. James is not someone Robert wants anywhere near his house, but I didn't have a choice. The appliances need to get on the truck.

"Hi, James."

"Hey, I'm almost there," James responds.

"Okay, thank you so much for bringing them to me. Robert's not going to like it, so I think it's best if we just stay outside and have the movers transfer them over."

I'm not sure why he's threatened by my real dad's side of the family. We have not been able to have them in our lives since Robert made his entrance.

"I'm so sorry about this, James."

"It's okay. I understand. I'll see you in about ten minutes."

Like a gazelle, Micah runs through the garage and down the driveway. Grami's right behind. At the doorway, she looks at her feet, and then carefully steps down into the garage.

Micah jumps in front of me. "Hey Ang, who was that?" We embrace. His youth is intoxicating and eases my stress.

"James is on his way."

"It'll be okay." He squeezes tighter.

With his arm still around me, we walk to Grami.

"Well, are you ready?" I manage a wry smile, leaning in to kiss her.

She raises an eyebrow, nodding her head.

Leaving Grami in the driveway, Mic and I walk to the truck. Tommy and John unload boxes, bubble wrap, furniture blankets and dollies.

I pull John aside. "I think we'll start upstairs."

Loaded with boxes and bubble wrap, they follow me inside. Room-by-room I explain what needs to be packed. I can't think through what I want or don't want, so I take everything. I tell them to empty Mom's closets and dresser and even bathroom stuff. I empty the walls of her mother and child pictures. I walk them through the attic and take her quilt stuff and Christmas decorations.

Where's that stain glass window she made?

Then I freeze... in front of the rug she made. It's a spiral rug woven, coiled and stitched together using strips of old clothes and blankets and scraps. The end coils in a nearby basket, unfinished. I can't bring myself to take it. I'm removing everything that was hers. I still feel her presence. If I continue, if I remove all her things, she will disappear. The unfinished rug remains.

"What's he doing here?" Robert yells up the stairs.

Oh, no. Has ten minutes passed already? I wanted to be down there. Maybe even keep him from knowing that James was here. I've spent so much of my energy over the years trying to manage Robert's moods. Trying to keep it all positive. So, he can't hurt Mom with his outbursts. Unsuccessful once again. At least Mom's not hurting anymore.

"He's dropping off my washer and dryer." I'm down the hall and at the bottom of the stairs before he can respond. I breeze by him, out the front door.

"Hi James. I'm so sorry. I meant to be out here when you got here."

"It's okay." James gives me a hug.

"Let me go get one of the guys." I turn to go inside as Micah walks out.

"It's okay, Ang. The two of us can do it."

"Great. Thanks guys. And thank you, James."

Back inside, Robert's on the phone.

"Can you come over? She's taking..."

Who's he talking to?

Upstairs on the landing, I freeze again. Her book, *Marine Survival Manual*. But that's where she put it. She touched it last. If I move it, if I touch it, she will disappear. I shake out the fear I can't face, heedlessly walking by.

The guys are making quick work of the upstairs. I find a few more things to add as boxes are stacked on the landing, at the front door and in the grass. Each time I pass by the book, it becomes easier.

We move downstairs. I take some of Mom's kitchen things, things that remind me of my childhood. The dining room table and sideboard originally belonged to my great-grandma, then to Grami and then to Mom... now to me.

"You're taking the table?" Robert stands, arms crossed, with his parents on either side.

So that's who he called.

I have my people. I guess he needs his. They pretend they're here to say goodbye, but I know the truth.

"It's not yours. It was handed down three generations." In my mind, it's not even a question. I nod to the movers who grab either end.

Like he's in charge, Robert marches out behind them, keeping a keen eye on everything going out the door. His demeanor intimidates the untrained and unsuspecting prey that would dare to wander into his web.

I stand in the empty room, lost inside my head. It's almost over. I close my eyes, slump over and exhale. A hand intertwines with my fingers. I know it's Grami without opening my eyes. Her soft loose skin sends a soothing warmth up my arm, through my neck and rests behind my eyes. They softly open.

"What about that?" She motions to a picture on the wall.

That same fear wells up. Mom will disappear. I won't be able to feel her anymore.

"No. We're taking so much."

But it's not any picture. Grami gave that picture to Mom. It's a young girl standing in a field next to a lamb. According to Grami, it's a picture of me.

I leave the room, swiping Mom's tack hammer off the wall. Another special item that swipes another piece of her out of this house. Bit-by-bit she disappears.

The movers stand outside next to the truck. I go upstairs. One last look. On the landing, the book beckons. The cover curls over itself. Well read. Studied, in fact. Marked up. I scoop it up, stuffing it in my sling.

I leave through the empty dining room.

The girl on the wall is gone. As is my mother.

17
H-O-M-E

I drive past the large sign, "Cameron Creek Apartment Homes." Wow, I'm home. Passing by the four-tiered water fountain in the middle of the divided entry, surrounded by yellow and orange-red hot pokers shooting up amongst ornamental potato plant and mounds of petunias clumped together in reds, whites, purples and pinks. The years digging in the dirt with my mother are paying off.

I stuff the ache deep. Hidden. *Go away, I can't deal with you now. I'll tell you when it's time.*

Never.

The road narrows as I drive under an expansive portico reminding me of the Arc de Triomphe in Paris, the leasing office directly ahead. The truck carrying everything I own waits off to the side.

. . . . .

Keys to my new apartment home – my heart only sees the word home – in hand. The anticipation heightens... my first home. Home. I smile with childhood memories flooding my cerebral cortex. H-O-M-E. Mom says, "h-o-em-eee." I repeat, followed in quick succession by each of my siblings, spinning and dancing in a circle of ecstatic joy.

I turn the key... twist the handle... step inside. No... deflating, no...

Dark. Drab. Dull. A shadow instantly creeps into my soul. This was a mistake... a big mistake. What do I do? Nothing. I am powerless. Defeated. The ice-fire intensifies, sending menacing tentacles into my heart. My fingers tighten their grip around my thumb. The emotional weight manifests physically, arching my shoulders forward. My right arm shoots up to cradle and protect my sling-encased left arm as if that will do anything to stop any of this pain.

As with the ice-fire, I resign to endure, persevere.

No, no, no. You can't allow this to upset your carefully orchestrated balance of survival. It's okay, Angela. We're only here for six months until we can find a house, a real home. I soften my hold, allowing the left arm to fall a fraction of an inch. The fingers refuse to ease. A sliding glass door leads to the claustrophobic patio. The balcony overhead obscures all light. With the north wall completely in shadows, the only windows withhold all light.

Layer upon layer upon layer of white paint. Each time this apartment exchanges residence, a new layer is added to the previous. Whitewashed. Prosaic. Sterile. Lifeless.

Not the home I hunger for.

．　　●　　．　　●　　．　　●

They said it was at the corner Cherry Lane and White Settlement. The only church close to this intersection is First Baptist Church but it's the wrong Baptist church and not actually on the corner. I drive a block in every direction and find more churches, most are Baptist, one is even called Faith Baptist Fellowship. Pretty close but not quite. I expand the search another two blocks... First Assembly of God, Fort Worth Baptist Temple, Wyatt Drive Baptist Church, Spirit of Truth Ministries, St. Peter Catholic Church and West Freeway Church of Christ. A church on every corner but still not the one I'm looking for.

Returning to the intersection of Cherry and White Settlement, I hesitantly venture into First Baptist Church, a large multi-leveled brick building, aged and weathered yellow bricks. This place has been here awhile and reeks of tradition. I'm greeted with a smile and a handshake. I match his plastic smile. I don't like church, but aren't you supposed to go to church? And like it? Kinda like medicine.

"Do you know where Faith Community Baptist Church is? My friends told me that it was at this intersection, but your church is the only one I can find." I turn sideways towards the door. I am not staying. I just need help.

"No, I'm sorry. But you are welcome to worship with us." He puts a not-so-gentle hand against my back directing me towards the sanctuary.

A knot forms in my gut. I noticeably shrink away from his touch. "No, thanks. I'll just keep looking." I desperately pivot counter-clockwise and am out the door before he can respond. Adrenaline floods my heart as if it's going to break through my rib cage and plop out onto my lap. Blinded, I sit in my truck. Breathing. Just breathing.

The adrenaline retreats, settling the heart back into its allotted space. I don't understand why that affected me so completely, but I don't have time to figure it out. The clock on my radio reads 10:23. I'm going to be late. I hate being late. I push it down. Shake it out. Dismiss it and pull back out onto White Settlement Road.

The stoplight is green, but the intersection is empty. I scan each of the four corners. A two-story, unmarked, brick building is to my left, First Baptist Church adjacent. The Bingo Hall on my right. The corner ahead on my right is filled with overgrown trees and bushes. Only one left. The first five hundred feet is an empty lot, littered with garbage and broken, weeded concrete, folded over itself. The decrepit, crumbling strip-mall starts with a furniture store bursting at the seams. The sidewalk is piled with couches and beanbags, rustic benches and tables. The furniture inside is stacked high upon each other, pressing against the broad storefront windows.

A sprawling live oak obscures a small white sign with green writing. Faith Community Baptist Church shares a modest alcove with Kevin's Hometown Furniture. Cracked and crumbling bricks expose the pillars' concrete core. I enter through the double-glass doors.

In stark contrast to its neighbor, the small foyer is bright, simple, fresh. No pretense. The veneer of the entrenched church across the street and around the corner is absent.

Could this be home?

.   .   .   .   .

I meet my realtor, Julie, out front. Another house in a long succession. Every weekend, and even during the week, she brings more options. But this one is a little different. I asked to see this one. I drive around Fort Worth most evenings searching for the perfect neighborhood. Very short drive to work – within ten minutes – that's a deal breaker. Trees are required. Variety and character, I can't breathe without it. And this one's got it in spades. The roads curve and meander up-and-down the hills. I even get lost. There's a lake just two blocks away. Every house, built in the fifties, is unique. The live oaks, more than three feet wide, stretch out over the neighborhood.

The house sits sixty feet from the road behind a lush, juicy-green yard at the bottom of a steep hill. Well, it's steep for someone from flat Indiana farmland. An expansive red oak tree on the right and a row of three young live oaks on the left. The deep coo of a dove welcomes me. I breathe it in. That coo takes me back to Francesville, Indiana and is the first sign that I'm h-o-em-eee. The house itself is white brick with just one large window divided into three panels. The bottom edge, eight feet above the ground; the top angles up, following the roof line. The chimney juts out, topped off with a custom, copper cap, beautifully oxidized in a rich patina.

The front porch, just wide enough for the door and glass side panel. The black door is inset with an antique, stain-glass window. A delicate design of leaded-glass in greens, reds and blues that resembles a flaming-red tulip. Mom's stain glass tools are tucked away in one of those boxes stacked high in my spare bedroom. I got a two-bedroom just for the boxes filled with my mother.

The modest entry opens into... wow. My jaw drops. Eyes pop open. The east wall is windows, just windows. Floor to ceiling windows. The vaulted ceiling rises all the way to the roof. Is that like fifteen or twenty feet? Light sketches and scribbles and scratches, dancing around the room. What more is there to see? This is h-o-em-eee.

Just as my heart threatens to fill with joy, a weight fills it instead. I panic. Fear overwhelms. Threatened by joy? Wow, trauma has so completely overwhelmed my body, feeling anything scares the crap out of me. Gotta keep the status quo. Guard dogs return to their post. Looking over at Julie, I don't think she notices. Good.

Carefully gathering up the illusion of emotion, I muster a smile and exclaim, "This is incredible, Julie. I need to put an offer on this place."

.   .   .   .   .

A whirlwind of activity fills my new home. My co-workers, whom all have quickly become my family, empty their trucks and fill my house. Half-open pizza boxes stack up in the kitchen. Red SOLO cups dot the rooms.

Andy and Kurt set up my bed. Buzz and Mike pile boxes filled with my mother in the middle bedroom, transferred from one spare bedroom to another. I stand in the dining room, frozen, watching the boxes stack higher and higher, filling the room. Oh, Mommy, you would love this house. I can't wait to call her and tell her about the windows, the light, the huge backyard, the amazing trees and the birds. A blue jay lands on the birdfeeder on the other side of my wall of windows.

No, she doesn't have a phone number. The lava tentacles invade my heart.

I try to breathe, closing my eyes to break the link. Tentacles recede. I think I'll just keep her in there for now. Can't upset my balance. Rotating clockwise to face the living room, I open my eyes. Mark looks like he needs a job.

"Mark, can you hang this over the fireplace."

I point to a painting I purchased in Vienna, Austria. Well it's a print of a painting and at first glance it's just a bouquet of flowers, but it gets interesting at close inspection. A lizard crawls out from under the carved, terracotta vase and eats one of the eggs stolen from a nest in the bottom left corner. Moths, bees and butterflies rest on various flowers, some with little droplets of water. A marble statue looks on from the distance.

He lifts the painting, revealing a Mother's Day gift, a stack of four large black and white photos, framed with a white mat and black frame. Back in another lifetime, when I was a photography major at IU, I made those for my mom. Her four babies smile at her. Now they're mine, again. I made these for you, Mom. Now I must hold on to you, keep you alive, keep your love alive. We've got a big backyard to fill with flowers, just give me some time, we'll do it together.

Happiness and sadness war inside. I feel her, yet she's not here. This is a major step in my life, and she is not here. I have family surrounding me, supporting me, but they are merely a facsimile.

The last items inside. Pizza gone. Standing in my barren, white garage, I wave to my facsimile family.

Alone.

Silent.

Content.

Doors and windows stand open. The garage forms a tunnel sucking through the soft, warm breeze. A jasmine-scented zephyr swoops through my soul taking with it the weight I've carried. The weight Robert brought into our lives.

For the first time in my life, I am free.

I am home.

I swing my arms out, exclaiming...

Wait. Looking down, only one arm takes flight. Confused, almost in shock. I forget for a second. Oh, I don't care, shaking it off. That thing is going to remain plastered to my chest, encased in a sling. Paralyzed. I'm not going to let it ruin this moment.

"H-o-em-eee."

Part Two

The Egglet

Perched high above the reach of predators, an eagle's nest is a massive 8 foot deep platform.

He found him in a desert land
And in the wasteland, a howling wilderness;
He encircled him, He instructed him,
He kept him as the apple of His eye.

Deuteronomy 32:10

18
A Gentle Wobble

The two-year anniversary unceremoniously passed a month ago. I'm still broken. How do I mark that kind of anniversary? Celebrate my mother's death at my hand? Celebrate my paralysis? What can I say? What can anyone say? Sorry. I'm praying for you. Are there words, or better yet, actions?

At the behest of friends and perhaps one such action, I pull up in front of 1623 Oakbrook Court to pick out my new puppy.

Pausing before I open the door. I'm not sure this is a good idea. I can't even take care of myself. I could leave. Yes, maybe I should wait another year. Oh, I'll look. It can't hurt to just look, right?

Carefully. Hesitantly. I walk up the driveway and through the garage. A smitten little girl cuddles with one as I step past the whelping box and into the backyard. Was I ever that free? Not weighed down by the harshness of this world. Purely in the moment.

I'm greeted by a sea of plump, black furballs scampering about.

Not sure if I want a girl or a boy, I lift the first one high into the sky, blinded by the noon sun. A little boy. I bring him down and bury my face into his soft warm belly. Wow, I could get used to this. This warmth. This love. Another heartbeat in my life.

Suddenly, a shiver shoots up. Starting at my foot, all the way up my leg, through my spinal cord and out the top of my head.

What was that? A soft, warm pressure on my thonged foot.

I rotate the puppy, tucking him into the crook of my elbow.

Big brown eyes look up, penetrating the shell I've been living in for the last two years. God opens His fingers ever so slightly, letting in a soft stream of light. The shell doesn't crack, but I awaken from a deep slumber. My eyes open. The egg gently wobbles as my body unfurls.

Her eyes pierce into my soul and take something. Something very precious. Something I've protected and guarded for a very long time. What is it about this little black puppy with the big brown eyes that I trust so completely?

Surprised. No. Shocked as the sensation shoots through my heart. Is that love?

Those eyes penetrate past the callused wall. She quietly sits. Our gaze locks. A silent conversation. An intimate connection. She knows me better than I know myself.

I blink as she jumps on my leg. Intrigued, I place the little boy in the grass. His tiny legs sink deep into the lush Saint Augustine pile. And scoop up the little girl. The one that took something from me.

I cup her tiny head in my hand as her body drapes down my right forearm. She climbs up my chest, attacking my face.

The connection is complete.

She picks me.

The sensation burning deeper into my heart is way too overwhelming. The crisp callus cracks open and breaks off in small chunks.

I feel. For the first time in two years, I feel. Since that time in the ICU when my aunts confirmed my mother was gone, and I wrapped the shell around, protecting my heart, I feel.

It's confusing and scary. I don't like it. She snuggles close. Her wet nose touches the scar on my neck. Or was it the deep scar running down the center of my heart? Another chill shivers through my body. I panic. Almost like she's too hot, I jerk her away, and she jumps to the ground. She scampers off, and I'm frozen. But I can't pull my eyes away, following her as she jumps and tumbles with a few of her siblings.

No. No. No. In a panic, my stomach twists and turns. I can't lose her in the sea of black fur. Running, no leaping over, I gather her up.

To free my only useful hand, I tuck her into my sling and dig out the twenty-five dollars required to make her mine.

We wind our way through the garage, down the driveway and back to my truck. What just happened? I haven't changed, although I'm not the same person I was a few minutes ago. I'm stronger. Well not me. This little black Labrador retriever has strength for the both of us.

A towel-lined box in the front seat doesn't contain this lively pup. Before I get the keys in the ignition, she's curled up in my lap.

The ache in my heart softens as the minutes tick away. My fingers nest in soft, warm fluff. Those eyes continue to reach down into my soul and pull it out. The pain. The fear. The panic. She holds it safely for me.

Driving home is different. The truck feels different. The cushion wraps around my thighs. There are ridges on the steering wheel. Has the sky always been a luscious marine blue?

And my front yard. Wow, I love that juicy green. Opulent white garage walls. Everything is fuller. More alive. Vivid. Voluptuous colors. Plush sounds.

More callus cracks off the shell.

Opening the car door, she's so excited. I'm not sure but think this is what cheeks feel like with you smile. The skin creases together and my mouth fills with cool oxygen. I intertwine my fingers with her front legs stopping her before she has a chance to jump out. That drop is too high for my little puppy.

What is this strange feeling? Happiness?

Stuffing her safely in my sling, we slide out of the cab. She scampers out just as I bend over.

She circles around my feet, sitting down right in front of me. "You're my mommy. Let's get started."

"Okay, little one, let me show you around." Leading her to the back door. She tries to climb up the step but it's too big, and she topples backward. Was that another smile?

Bending down, I give her a little boost. She runs across the landing and tumbles back off the next step. This girl is fearless. She turns and looks at me. "Please help."

Smiling. And then something like a chuckle. "Here you go." Pushing her tiny body up the last step.

She runs outside and summersaults down the step and into the yard. Her tiny legs get lost in the grass but that doesn't stop my girl. She jumps and leaps and skips and then collapses, exhausted, at my feet.

I am beginning to imagine the adventures we will have together. The shell cracks a little more. I'm beginning to imagine a future.

Bending down, I slide my hand under her belly and lift her to my eyes. "What is your name, little one?"

She licks my nose, placing a paw on my cheek. That soft pad reaches down deep establishing an unbreakable link. Our hearts beat as one.

"Okay, let's go inside."

Plopping down on the ground, I tumble, and she climbs all over me.

I toss a ball across the room.

She returns, bouncing the ball into my lap, "again, again." Her body shakes with excitement.

Over and over and over again. Until she deflates exhausted on my tummy.

She sleeps. I stare, infatuated. In love. Oh, my sweet baby. What did I do without you? I don't remember what life was like just a few hours ago... without you.

I tie helium balloons around her neck. I think I laugh out loud. She barrel rolls and rubs her head along the floor but eventually gives up and sits in front of me. "Please help."

"Okay, little bug, here you go." Untying the balloons and releasing them to the ceiling.

We take trips outside every few minutes. "Go potty."

The third time my brilliant little girl runs over to the door and returns, sitting in front of me. "I have to go potty."

"Good girl. Let's go." I smile as she stubbles over those two steps.

The luscious marine blue mixes with sensuous burgundy, succulent citron and extravagant salmon. The clouds twist and turn and flow as the sun approaches the horizon. The burgundies deepen and darken. Onyx and coal and ebony replace the citron and champagne.

My heart is full.

We are exhausted. I put her to bed and retire to mine. Just a few minutes pass, it starts as a faint whimper. Then the pitch rises. I bring her into my bed, but she won't settle. I take her back out. She curls up in a little ball but cries as soon as I walk away. Her head bobbles as she tries to stay awake.

I lie down next to her. "What is your name, little bug?" Resting my hand on her.

We cuddle. We talk. We love.

Before night turns to day, she releases the secret.

"My name is Mattie."

The shell cracks open.

Pause & Breathe

Scan your body.

Sit in a chair. Feel your feet on the ground. Place your hands on your abdomen. Feel it move with each breath. Your body is alive. It is protecting and nourishing you.

Dogs, in my experience, are perfect healers, but humans are designed to need human connection.

Don't worry about it. Those precious connections will show up in the most unexpected ways. Just be open.

But, not everyone is worthy of your heart. Some will hurt, not heal. Some will bring their own needs to the relationship and expect you to get over it.

Run from them.

Love is being the person who will just hold the pain.

Flying Lesson.
Find choice souls to hold it. Dogs work.

19
Slogging

"How are you?" With a genuine smile, my friend leans over the pew, arms ready to embrace.

Oh, the question. I hate the question. I can't lie or tell the truth. I return the smile and the embrace, my broken, one-armed version. I hate the incomplete hug. My arm withers, helpless, at my side. The question floats between us as the hug lingers. She wants to know but that makes it worse. I can't lie. And the truth? How many times can she hear it and not tire of me?

The longer the embrace, the worse it gets. Does she feel it? My agony. My pain. My despair. My body sinks into her love as my smile falls away. I could give the standard, cultural response. *Fine, how are you?* Or I could give some sort of godly, churchy response. *God isn't giving me more than I can handle.*

I want to scream, NO. I want to die. I want the pain to stop.

In the hug, I'm safe. I don't have to choose.

Ooh, there's the final squeeze, signaling the end. I return it and release. What do I say? How do I answer?

Why does this still hurt so deeply? I want to get over it. Just go on. Live my life. Forget.

The pain will not allow me to forget. My hand is locked in the moment when ice begins to burn. Every second of my life, it is frozen in the ice-fire. The invisible flames lick the block of ice anchoring my dead arm to the ground. As if that's not enough, a stranger comes up behind me, without warning or permission, knife in hand. He cuts open my bicep, jabbing the tip into the humerus, raking a deep, rusty groove down the bone. Every thirty seconds. For forty-eight, uninterrupted hours, the torture continues, every other week.

What is my answer?

Well my hand is a block of ice-fire. They already know that. Why waste precious energy telling them again? *The knife pain isn't so bad, today.* They might rejoice and think I'm okay. *My heart hurts. Aches. Deep down, I just want to die.* There's nothing they can do, and it might elicit some meaningless platitude or guilt-inducing Bible verse. *I really want my mommy. I just can't get over the guilt.* Nope, that will get the standard. It's not your fault. That's why it's called an accident.

More ladies gather around. My struggle for the correct answer turns into an awkward silence.

What do I say? What do I say? Oh, crap, I don't know what to say.

"I'm not okay." I blurt out. "I can't keep saying I'm okay."

They stare. They just stare. Can you blame them? What are they supposed to say? Yep, I just threw a bomb into the sanctuary, leaving everyone dumbfounded and mute.

I should have brought Mattie. Why didn't I bring Mattie? She is so strong. I would be so much stronger with her. Run. I can run. Yes, I should run. C'mon, legs move.

My feet are glued to the carpet.

Laugh it off. Dismiss it. Tell 'em you're okay.

The words are stuck somewhere in my gut. I should have stayed home. Why do I even leave the house? Just me and Mattie. Everything is so much better with Mattie. She understands. Well, more accurately, she doesn't need to understand. She accepts me for who I am, bulbous, hairy warts and all. With Mattie, I can breathe.

Without her, grief invades every cell. I taste it. It is my only nourishment. It's all I feel. It burns out every desire, every care, all I love and hate. I'm reduced to a dense ball of guilt and fear and hopelessness and anger and despair.

Like the manna of the wandering Israelites, I eat my daily portion. I digest the mystery, the manna, the what is it? Every morning I gather it. I ingest it. I wear it. It is my cloak, my armor. It is the only way I survive. The wilderness is my home. Life is a joyless absence, eating away all memories, old and new. The spell is full and complete, preventing any hope of escape.

I buy food simply because I'm supposed to. But, I don't eat. It rots in the refrigerator, on the counter and in the cupboard. I plan to eat. I read about eating. But, I don't eat. Unless I'm fed. Unless I'm invited to dinner. Unless I go out with friends.

But somehow, I'm nourished. I don't waste away. I gain weight. I welcome the layer of fat. It thickens the wall. It fortifies the armor, as I feel my way through the treacherous path set before me, slogging in the murk and mud. I need a guide. A hand. A map. An understanding word. Someone to say, "You're going the right way. I'm right here next to you."

These friends try, but I need someone who understands without explanation. I don't have the energy to explain.

. . . . .

I bring Mattie. Can't do this without her. She hops up to the front seat, sits, turning towards me.

Bright eyes, at the ready. "What are we doing, Mom? What, what, what? I'm so excited." She leans over, nudging my hand with her nose.

We sit in the parking lot. The neon-green brochure crumples under her weight.

Grief Recovery Class

March - April 2003, Wednesday Night 7 PM

Altamesa Church of Christ

Will they understand or just paste a Bible verse on top like a band-aid? That fixes nothing. My heart aches. I can't breathe. I'm lost. When will Jesus rescue me? Another cold nose to the hand.

"Okay, we're going but you need to hold me up."

The same neon-green is taped to the door. Inside, narrow tables form a square. Each chair has a neon-blue booklet and a sharpened number two pencil. Kleenex boxes and water pitchers at each table. The ceiling sits a little too low, fluorescence lights buzzing. Nineteen-eighties carpet matted down to the concrete.

Engulfed by a smile and hug.

"Welcome, I'm Mary Jane Coolidge."

She releases and sure enough, her name tag confirms it. This is Mary Jane Coolidge. More importantly, her eyes tell it all. Behind the bubbly, this woman understands pain. Right beside her, Glenn Coolidge. Must be her husband. Envelopes me in another hug.

Hugs. Can they feel it? My brokenness? My paralyzed arm?

"And who is this?" Glenn bends down, rubbing Mattie's ears.

Good, they don't seem to notice. My beautiful girl takes the attention away from me. Breaks the ice. Opens the conversation. Gives me room to breathe.

"This is Mattie. Don't worry, she'll behave herself. I'll just put her in the back corner."

Mattie sniffs Glenn and then Mary Jane.

"I don't doubt it. She is gorgeous."

We get our name tags, Mattie too, although it falls off her silky black fur. She curls up in the corner, and I take my seat. Written on the neon-blue, *Week 1: Beginning the Walk*. We go around the table, telling our stories. Stories of loss and pain, grief and anger, despair and regret. People who know pain. Yes, I can rest, just a bit, as we suffer together.

I return every week. Sometimes without Mattie. When the five weeks end, I return to the next class. A new group of grievers. A new crop of stories. Mary Jane Coolidge invites me to the next class and the next class and the next class. I tell my story again and again and again to those who don't need an explanation.

"Feel your pain. Grieve at your own pace." Mary Jane Coolidge stands beside me, well beside Mattie, beside me.

Pause & Breathe

Scan your body.

We've been through hell and survived. We see that our own bodies have ways to cope with trauma. We've found a dog or a friend or a support group or a nice quiet place in nature or a quiet corner of our home.

Whatever and wherever you feel safe.

Now, it might be time to feel. To be present in your pain. Can you risk it?

Lie down on your back, knees bent, feet flat on the floor. Feel your body being supported by the ground below and gravity above. Breathe. Rest your arms at your side. Inhale. Feel your belly expand, then your ribs and lastly your shoulders rise. Exhale. Shoulders relax, ribs rest, belly sinks in. Again. Belly. Ribs. Shoulders. Exhale. Shoulders, ribs, belly. Again.

Move your attention to your skin. Is there a breeze? Feel the soft weight of your clothes. Soften your eyes. Your jaw. Where are you holding? Does it hurt? Adjust your weight so that you're a bit more comfortable.

Feel what you feel. Be present in your pain.

Love by being present with those who suffer.

Flying Lesson.
Be present in your skin.

20
Dark-n-Damp

The front tires roll up over the curb. After I give it a little gas, the back ones strain over and sink into the soil. Sandstone boulders weigh down the bed, testing the suspension, but my little black Chevy can take it.

I thread the truck between the stone wall and the three live oaks lined up along my driveway, past the garage, through the fence and into the backyard. I drive straight to the back and put it into reverse, backing up to my hole. Mattie watches, sitting patiently on the other side. I've been working on this hole for two years. These boulders are the last touch. I should be filling it with water tonight, if all goes as planned.

That's a big if, since this arm just hangs at my side. I call him Little Guy. My brain doesn't recognize him as part of me. I'm legitimately concerned about how the biggest one will get to the island in the middle. But it's the coolest part so I don't have a choice.

All done with my mother in mind. Gotta find a way to be with her without continually returning to that icy intersection. She would love it here in my backyard with Mattie Mae.

My garden starts with a basic pond kit from Home Depot, consisting of an eight-by-ten-foot, black, rubber liner, a five hundred gallon-per-hour pump with two fountain heads and a floating, solar, frog light, for $97.88. The instructions are on a single-sided, photocopied, crumpled piece of paper with four simple steps and five required items.

Rope. Flat Head Screwdriver. Edging Material (i.e. rock). Long Nails. Garden Shovel.

C'mon, really? You dig a hole, put the liner in and fill with water. I understand the rock and shovel and maybe even the rope to mark out the shape. I would rather just dig the hole, organically creating the shape. But nails and a screwdriver? I don't think so. I stuff the sheet of paper back into the box and get my shovel.

The soil is not soil. The boiling, summer sun turned it to rock. Sweat drips off me as the sun sets and the temperature flirts with dipping into the nineties. My hole is hardly taking shape. That is to say, it does have shape, not much depth.

The box with the crumpled instructions, rubber liner, pump and solar frog are stored in the shed as I settle in for a summer of digging. It's soothing, mindless, sweaty work with my Mae and my mom. My Mae watches from the shade.

Mom. Is she here? Watching? I'm doing this for her. Well not really for her, but more to help remember or honor her. Oh, I don't know why. *I want you to see this. To experience this. This place I've made for myself. Are you proud of me? Or angry? I'm sorry. I didn't mean... to...*

I can't even let the words form in my brain. Eyes crunch tight as my fingers lose their grip on the handle. The shovel bounces off the ground, flinging little balls of rock-dirt into the air. My knees start to buckle but Mattie's, strong body presses against them. Her nose pushes up against my hand.

My eyes pop open. "Oh, hi Mae. Thanks, baby." Her attention and care are ever-present. I crumple to the ground to receive my Mattie medicine.

. . . . .

The Texas summer stretches into November, but by Christmas, the naked hole lies abandoned. A deep scar matching the one in my soul. Micah's visit reignites my resolve. Two days later, he stands, like a statue, hand high atop the handle, foot resting on the spade. Proud of our finished hole. We fill the bottom with a layer of sand, place the liner and rocks. With water, the hole transforms into a pond. A place for life to grow. A place for my heart to rest. A trip to PetSmart for a dozen comet goldfish and my pond is complete. Or is it?

The ache in my heart remains. Mom doesn't visit. Who could blame her? It looks like a random disturbance in a half acre of grass. My work is not complete. This garden for my mother is not complete.

It needs a waterfall. And flowers. And trees. And an island. It must be tripled in size with waterlilies and bright orange fish. Turtles, snails and frogs. Big belching bullfrogs.

A new shape marked out in red spray paint. A new kit purchased from pond outlet dot com. And a tiller. This is too big and too deep for one-armed me and a shovel. The tiller pulverizes the winter soil and that incessant ache into submission.

The new pond kit spread out on the grass. Instructions are in a booklet with too many parts to count and steps that require my adherence. I place the skimmer in its two-by-two-by-two foot hole on the south end and the biofalls filter at the north end. They connect with flexible tubing running in a trench around the pond.

The felt lining goes down first, covering my hole and the layer of play sand, followed by the rubber liner. All the pieces are secured together with fish-safe, silicone sealant. The entire ecosystem is then covered with rocks. Big rocks. Little rocks. Round rocks and flat rocks. I cover the bottom with river rocks and stack rocks up the sides. I make trip after trip after trip to the rock-n-stone yard. They weigh my Chevy pickup before and after I pick the perfect rocks.

Black rocks. Red, white and yellow rocks. Sandstone and limestone and granite and lava. They all have their place in my garden. And I use my feet, hips and core to roll and slide each one. Little Guy tries to help.

The water pump is housed at the bottom of the skimmer under filter material and a debris net, pumping the water at four thousand gallons per hour to the biofalls. The water enters at the bottom of the biofalls, rising through lava rock, sand and more filter material and spilling out over the front edge, through and around the carefully placed rocks forming my waterfall.

Twenty feet away I dig out the sod for my vegetable garden, two three-by-ten foot rectangles connected by a flagstone walkway down the middle and bordered with red sandstone blocks. The soil is dark and damp following the spring rains, asking for life to take root.

At the nursery, I fill up my plastic trays with cucumbers, peppers, tomatoes, sugar snap peas, mint and marigolds. I round the corner to find the perennials. Coreopsis. *Oh, Mom, look, there's the coreopsis. We loved us some coreopsis, didn't we?* Delicate yellow flowers atop spindly green stalks, screaming to be noticed.

. . . . .

Popping open the hatchback, we pull plastic trays out of my Subaru. Mom hands me the last one, spindly coreopsis full of blossoms ready for the sun and soil. We work as one. But it's not work. This is fun. We dig. We plant. We laugh. We find the perfect spot for each little gem. Some will grow tall. Others will be short and fat. Some will have screaming, bright, crazy flowers. Others will fruit. There are tiny, delicate petals and sharp, three-inch thorns. Some need to be protected. Others can defend themselves.

. . . . .

Oh Mom, where are you? I need your protection.

A peach tree. Three pomegranate trees. Red raspberries next to the shed. And rhubarb against the back fence under a fifty-year-old oak is the most important. Mom's going to need it for my birthday rhubarb pie.

Five white Crape Myrtle form a line along the east fence. A Mexican Fan Palm planted on the west side of the pond balances two maroon Crape Myrtle on the east.

Mom remains elusive.

My spade cuts deep into the dark and damp, searching for the elusive. The boiling Texas sun soothes my shivering soul stuck at that icy intersection. The only place I can find my mother.

I drive my body. I force my muscles, even paralyzed ones, to push and pull. I work the soil. Thrusting the metal blade, Little Guy holds on for dear life, crying out. Each thud into the black sends Knife gleefully up the radial nerve. I bury Little Guy deeper and deeper. I refuse to see the disability. I refuse to give in to the paralysis. This is not me. It will never be me. I will fight till he's back to normal, or I die.

I do not rest. My eyes are blind to the beauty I created. I am lost.

Lost in the dark and damp.

21
First Flinch

The routine. Five years now. Three days a week, every week. Without words, we submit to the routine. I recline on the treatment table, disappearing inside. Stabilizing my shoulder with her left hand, Gwen lifts Little Guy.

The routine continues, as Gwen progresses through the stretches. I like this part. I get to relax. Disappear. Nothing's expected of me. I don't have to fight, fight to survive, fight to live. For a few precious minutes.

Then the physical therapy exercises begin. Gwen moves my arm while telling my brain to do its job. But it can't. This thing is dead. Paralyzed. Completely immobile, dangling at my side. It yanks at my shoulder. It endlessly pulls at the muscles and tendons. The pain. Oh, I don't even know what to say about the pain.

Exercises, if that's what you want to call them. My brain is not moving anything. Gwen is doing all the work.

"Bend your arm." She instructs, while tapping my bicep.

I focus. Deep inside my brain, I try to send a signal to my arm. *Bend!* I feel the neurons. They fire all around my brain. They're like little feathers, floating and connecting at the speed of an electron. But I need to find one particular neuron, just one that will send a signal to my bicep.

Bend!

Why doesn't she lift? She always lifts it for me. Does she know something I don't?

Doctor Kline said it would take five years. Well, it's been five years. *Bend!* It will take five years for the nerves to grow to your muscles, he said. *Bend!* You will need to retrain your brain to send a signal through new connections, he cautioned. *Bend!* Your muscles will have atrophied. This process will be long and difficult. You will need to fight.

I am fighting. I'm here, aren't I? For five years, I've been here.

. . . . .

Another waiting room, my fourth this week.

A sticker, on a clipboard, filled in with the appropriate data. The woman behind the counter hands me another clipboard. Paperwork. So much paperwork. My story doesn't fit within the standard questions. I carry my story with me. It is written on my face and in my bones. It is hole-punched and organized in a bright, red, Presstex binder. Each surgery, test and therapy further subdivided with color-coded tape flags.

Submitting to the routine, muscles wasted away in pointless therapy, while I waited six months for Doctor Kline to transfer nerve function. I did my three-month internment in the California HMO system. And nine more while back at Purdue.

Now, settled in Fort Worth, I need this to work. It can't be just any therapists.

I need to find my team. So, the paperwork. The clipboard. The endless questions.

What is your major complaint?

My arm doesn't move. My hand is on fire. My shoulder feels like it's being pulled out of socket. Knife rakes down my arm every thirty seconds. I can't sleep because I'm in agony and a comfortable position remains elusive. My head feels too heavy, and my neck aches all the time. Eating requires too much energy. My heart is crushed beyond hope. Which *major complaint* do I choose?

How long have you had this condition?

Well that one's easy. Since January 24, 2001. I guess it's been about a year and a half. Oh, I'll just write the date.

Have you had this or similar conditions in the past?

Nope.

Do any positions make it feel worse? Or better?

I'm miserable. In agony. All the time. I have no idea how to answer those. Skip.

Is this condition: □ Improved □ Unchanged □ Getting worse

Did I mention miserable? All the time.

Is this condition interfering with your:
□ Work □ Sleep □ Daily Routine □ Other

Are you kidding me? Duh!

Other doctors or therapists who have treated <u>THIS</u> condition:

Not enough room on that line. And which condition are we talking about? I still can't answer the major complaint question above.

What do you think caused this condition?

Uh, I'm thinking maybe the accident.

List surgical operations and years:

Medications, dosage and frequency:

Ah, easy questions. Good thing I typed all that out. I'll just hand them a copy.

Have you been in an auto accident or had any other personal injury?
□ Y □ N □ Date

Isn't that what we've been talking about? Can't I just hand you my binder? Page one drains me. Emotionally exhausted, and I haven't even answered the questions. Doubting they read this, I hand it in as is and take my seat. Without looking, Becky, as her nametag informs, slips it into my chart. I knew it, not worth my meager energy. I'll save that for the therapist.

The desk wraps around, forming a small enclave and creating a barrier between the waiting room and the treatment area. Patients work on the various machines, a rower, a few arm bikes, a traction table and a stationary bike. Offices fill the glassed, back wall. The rest of the wall space is divided into private treatment rooms and a water therapy spa. There's a line of counter-height, single treatment tables and another row of knee-high, double tables.

Becky stands and motions to a woman behind the glass wall. She and another woman walk straight to me.

"Hi Angela. My name is Gwen, and this is Amy. Please come back."

"Okay, thanks." Gathering up my binder.

They glance down, then turn, leading me to the corner room.

"So, tell me your story." Amy invites.

How do they know there's more than a standard intake form can contain? Maybe it's the red folder. Or the worn-out sling. Or the look, I imagine, in my eyes, seeping out of my broken soul. They know, somehow, they know, and I give them my story. I risk wasting the very little energy I do not have.

Pulling open the red folder, I explain the accident, the surgery, the therapy, the medications and the pain. I tell it all. And I end with my questions.

"Are you interviewing us?"

Huh? I didn't think I was, but "yes, I guess I am."

They know, and I know. I have found my team.

. . . . .

Gwen taps my bicep. "This muscle, Angela. Move it."

I strain my neck, looking at where her fingers contact my skin. Her touch barely penetrates past the surface. My skin is numb, an impenetrable surface against the world.

Focusing on one neuron, I tense every muscle in my body.

C'mon Little Guy, you can do it. Bend!

It moves.

Wait, really? Did I just see that? It moved?

Well actually it jerks. A wild, amazing, crazy flinch. My brain moved my arm. My brain moved my arm. Holy Cow. My brain moved my arm!

Gwen drops it, rolls backward, jumps up and exclaims. "You did it." Arms flying.

Hers, that is. Mine are in shock. The room stops. The arm bike stops. The rower stops. The stationary bike, no one's on the stationary bike, but it stops too. The offices, behind the glass wall, empty.

"Her bicep flinched."

"Let me see." Amy comes in close.

Gwen rolls back over, gathering up my arm. "Can you do it again?"

She taps. I focus. The collective holds their breath. They are invested. Five years invested. Over two thousand hours, invested.

This is my team.

Little Guy sputters in response. A twitter. A twitch. Another flinch.

"Wow. Okay, I think we're done for the day. Way to go, Angela."

We hug. The one-armed, incomplete hug may soon be a distant memory. For now, each staff member gets their own, while Little Guy hangs at my side.

Pause & Breathe

Scan your body.

Look a little deeper this time. Rest your mind's eye on that place of greatest resistance. Is that safe? Maybe find another spot where you're able to navigate through the resistance.

Is it anger? Frustration? Sadness? What does it need? What will make you feel safe enough to face it?

There is nothing small about seeing my bicep flinch. But there is also nothing big about it. In my crazy, mixed-up viewpoint, where success happens when big things happen. When you fight and win. When you're a NASA engineer. When you get straight As, and not even one B is acceptable. When you get over your mother's death in the expected time. When you use a paralyzed arm like it was never damaged.

Not a flinch. C'mon, a flinch? Really? Rejoice for a flinch? And one that's not even repeatable.

Yes. I will say it again, yes. Feel it. And rejoice. Throw a party. Did you get out of bed today? Let you whole body smile.

Can you see the massive effort it takes for a trauma victim to simply breathe? Help them see the smallest triumph. And rejoice with them.

Flying Lesson.
Feel the triumph, no matter how small.

22
Caution: May Cause Drowsiness

Prescription bottles march down my kitchen counter. Time to sleep. Again. Such a vain prospect. What should we try tonight? Mattie sits beside me. Her knowing eyes give me... what? "What do you do for me, little girl?"

"I just love you, momma."

Yeah, that's it. Love. Leaning over, I press my face against hers. "Oh, I love you so much, baby." I breathe in, sucking her love deep into my chest.

Hydrocodone. Take two to three tablets at night as needed. Caution: May cause DROWSINESS. ALCOHOL may INTENSIFY this effect.

Amitriptyline. Take as needed. More of the same cautions.

Ultracet. Neurontin. Skelaxin. Lexapro. Oxycodone. Oxycontin. Tramadol. Ambien.

Take as needed. Really? What does that mean? I could take it all and never feel better. Maybe if I added the alcohol, it would help. I would sleep. Sleep through the pain.

I swallow my chosen cocktail and return to the couch, waiting for the effect to intensify. I'm not even sure which ones I chose. There's was a little round white pill along with a blueish oblong one and a few others. I hold off on the alcohol. I've only added that a few times over the years but just as an afterthought. Never a conscious choice to combine the two.

My body numbs with the passing of the clock. It ticks past midnight, bringing in the next day. Mattie paws the couch.

"Let's try, Mom."

I follow her down the hall and roll into bed.

"Oh Jesus, please give me just a few hours rest. Real rest. I'm so exhausted I don't even want to breathe." The silent plea gushes out of my heart, bouncing off the rib cage, returning with force, unanswered.

Unheard, shattering my hope

Do I honestly expect relief? When has that plea ever been heard? Maybe I should have chosen another drug combination. I could add a few more to the cocktail.

The pain incessantly nags. I roll on my left, jamming my hand between the mattress and my hip. The pressure. The warmth. Will it help at all? Oh, please help this time. Minutes pass without a change. I press my hip deeper. Could the pressure squeeze the pain out like toothpaste? Something needs to change. Now. Rolling on my right, I stuff my hand between my legs. Ice-fire is relentless. I squeeze tighter. My hand is locked in a solid block of ice, burning. Relentlessly burning.

Flinging the covers, my arm flies, uncontrolled, entangled in the comforter. I kick my legs free and want to jump out of bed, but my body doesn't cooperate. The pillows and blankets and paralyzed muscles suck me in like quicksand. Frustrated, I roll off the edge, crashing down on top of Mattie. Covers and pillows tumble down with me. Mattie leaps up, shakes and sneezes. She leans over, sniffing my face. "What are you doing, momma?"

"Sorry, baby. I can't handle this." My adrenalin fires, negating all the drugs I took. I push the covers away, heaving myself up. I cradle my arm, high against my heart. Pain. This is more than pain. My brain doesn't work. Blinded. All I feel. All I hear. All I see. All I know. All I am is the pain. I strangle my thumb in my right hand, fingernails digging into the skin.

In the dark, I don't even open my eyes. I see better with them closed anyway. Moving on instinct with sense memory, I retrieve the ace bandage and fleece glove, just the left one, from the dining room table. Slipping it over my hand, the fleece soothes Ice-fire until it returns, with a vengeance, twenty-three seconds later. I massage the thumb, stretching, squeezing, wrenching it back. For a few brief, precious moments, it helps.

Leaning over, I balance the forearm on the corner of the table. The hand hangs over the edge. I stuff the end of the ace bandage deep into the tight, black-fleece fist and wrap. Round and around. Tighter with each loop. Slowly the pain subsides. My brain works, and I see what I've just done.

Cut off the circulation. I loosen my grip, releasing the bandage to gravity. My heart, following the bandage, unravels to the carpet.

I need to loosen the wrap but the pain. I can't endure that pain. I wait, staring at my entombed hand, weighing the options. Agony? Or agony? I finally stand. The arm falls, bouncing against my hip. Returning to the couch, I drag that arm along. Mattie steps on the trailing bandage. Ice-fire returns before I settle in, before I press the power button, before I start another mindless episode.

Sleep will not come tonight.

. . . . .

Prescription bottles march.

My nightly routine begins again. Sleep? I shake my head, eyes close, deeply exhaling. The bottle with the little round white pills empties into my palm. Time for another refill. Time for another doctor's visit. Time for another trip to the pharmacy. I can't. The fatigue is paralyzing.

Mattie, my constant companion, leans against my thigh, looking deep into my soul. She knows.

. . . . .

Approaching the reception desk, the glass window slides open.

"Hello, Angela. I have your script right here."

I hate that they know me, but I love it at the same time. I don't want to be here. I don't want to need them. To need these drugs. But at least they know me.

"Thank you, but can I talk to the nurse, please."

"Um, okay. Let me go get her."

I fall into the black leather chair with cherry stained wooden armrests, eyes rolling back into my head. Confrontation. I need to ask for more. I hate it, but I can't keep doing this.

Calling Doctor Shank. Driving to Doctor Shank's office. Picking up my script. Driving to the pharmacy. Waiting in the pharmacy. Taking the drugs home. Lining up prescription bottles. Choosing my nightly drug cocktail.

Locked in the routine. Bound. More than my arm is paralyzed.

At the mercy of the doctors. The drugs. The pain. Every night. Weeks. Months. Years. No end in sight. No cure. No relief. Just managed pain. That is all I'm offered. But this is not managing. This is barely existing. If I can disrupt one small link in the chain, I could gain some control. Some freedom.

I'm so weighted down by this fierce world.

I hear the door open. Okay, Angela, it's time to open your eyes. All you can do is ask. I feel her sit next to me. C'mon. Open your eyes. Leaning forward, oh that takes so much effort, I look through pleading eyes.

"I can't do this anymore." I blurt out.

Susan pulls her shoulders back, eyes bulging. Hackles shoot up. "These are class A drugs. We can't call or fax it in. You need a physical prescription."

Oh crap. This is not going the way I meant. I shoot my hand up to my face, rubbing my weary eyes. Sliding my hand down over my nose, lips and chin, I brush her defensiveness away.

"No, wait a minute. I'm not attacking you. I understand the issue, but I need to figure out something else. I'm exhausted. In agony. I need the drugs, but I can't do this every month. It is killing me. Literally killing me."

Her body softens. I continue.

"Can you maybe mail the scrip to me or actually, a better option, to the pharmacy? Then all I have to do is pick it up."

"Yes, we can do that, but we still need to see you every three months. Just call us when it's time to refill, okay?"

Ah, I can breathe. Finally, I can get in some oxygen. "Thank you so much."

·   ·   ·   ·   ·

A year later, prescription bottles continue their march down my kitchen counter.

The little round white pills empty into my palm. Even this is getting tedious, but I make the call. I dial the phone. I ask for another script.

Mattie, ever present, Mattie Mae, leans and looks. Her weight, her eyes, her life, her presence makes my life survivable.

·   ·   ·   ·   ·

Another two years, the bottles marching down my kitchen counter remain.

I take two more little round white pills. I add the blue one and a big yellow one, then I make the call.

"Hi, Susan, I need another..."

Her voice breaks in. "I'm sorry, Angela, Doctor Shank passed away last week in a motorcycle accident. We can refer you to another neurologist."

No. What? I can't. I can't breathe. Or speak. I can't do this all over again. Train another doctor. Tell my story again. The story. Mom's story. The accident. My paralyzed heart... I mean... arm.

Mattie, still right beside me, leans in, heavy against my thigh. Her nose pushes up against that dangling hand. Only half of that hand feels her soft warm black fur. The other half is numb and on fire at the same time.

At the mercy of this vicious world. Everything ripped out from under my feet, once more. But there's nothing I can do. She's dead. I scribble down the names.

How do I gather the strength to call them?

I am dead inside. Everything that is me is dead. My heart beats. Lungs inhale oxygen. Cells process calories. Neurons fire in my brain to navigate the world around me.

But my soul is lost.

23
Within Normal Limits

As the lead flight test engineer for live missile testing, I drive north from El Paso deep into the New Mexico desert. "You need to stop at White Sands." I'm told. "It's breathtaking."

I step out onto sand. The harsh, black, gravel asphalt abruptly changes to blinding, white sand. Sound instantly drops away. Taking another step, the deep silence sucks the oxygen from my lungs. The next step forces my heart out of my chest and into my throat. The alien landscape stretches to the horizon. Every hair on my body shoots to attention.

Shivering in the boiling, bone-dry sauna, I continue deeper in. My knees weaken. The outside world feels miles away. My head spins. I widen my stance to balance, but my knees fold, sinking deep. The burning sand, now covering my naked thighs, does not support my weight. I rotate and softly recline, arms and legs outstretched, well just one arm. That other one remains plastered to my chest, cocooned in my worn-out sling. Sunlight burns bright red through closed eyelids. Still silence pulls me deep inside.

The effect is comforting, soothing. The pain in my hand, my arm, my neck, my shoulder blade. Oh, and in my head. It softens. The sauna seeps into my bones, covering the pain, like a salve. I let my soul quiet. I feel the heat. And the silence. It softens the pain I've tried so hard to keep in check. The walls drop, crashing and folding upon itself. Swallowed up by the sand. That ache in my heart, no longer protected by Ice-fire and Knife, rears its ugly head.

The demons overwhelm like a storm.

No. No. NO. Wait. Close the flood gates. WAIT.

"How much longer can you do this?" Despair asks.

Stop. This is why I don't let myself feel. I can still stop this. It's not too late.

"Don't worry, she'll give up any minute." Replies doubt.

"Yeah, all her doctors can't help. Her folder just gets thicker. Her complaints fall on deaf hears. She will never be free of her pain and fatigue."

You're right, but I'm not going to stop looking.

A friend loves Doctor Hoover. "You should go see him. He's a DO, and he treats the whole body. He treats each individual."

The drive is a little too far, but I'm desperate. I need help. Real help. He asks questions. He listens. He makes me believe. Doctor Hoover might just find the answer. I give my blood and wait. In agony. For three months. He finally has the results and an opening in his schedule. "Everything is within normal limits."

My heart deflates. I retreat inside and only hear every other word. "It might be your thyroid."

For three months, I obediently take the medications for hypothyroidism. I give more blood and wait in agony for the next available appointment. Nine weeks later, the results are "within normal limits."

But I'm exhausted. I can't sleep. I barely eat. Help me.

I don't tell him. I say okay. I say fine. I leave in despair.

"See, you will not get relief." Despair turns the knife.

Another friend can't say enough about Doctor Birdy. "She listens and treats holistically."

She fits me into her busy schedule. I slap down my red folder. I give her my story. I plead for her help. She orders the requisite blood tests, and I wait for one week. Just one week, but the results are not going to change just because another doctor orders the same tests.

Doctor Birdy decides to zero in my iron levels. They are within normal limits, but I'm treated for anemia.

I research diets to increase energy and metabolism. I print out recipes and shopping lists. I gather just enough energy to visit the grocery store, but there's not any left to cook. The food rots in the cupboard and the fridge. The printouts curl and yellow on my countertop.

Every woman in the metroplex knows of Doctor McWherter. I get on the waiting list.

My testosterone is a little low, I mean a tiny bit low. So, he prescribes testosterone, Armour Thyroid, compounded progesterone and B-12 shots. Then there's his supplements. I spend hundreds of dollars on his supplements. If I do it all, just as my doctor prescribes, I'm promised relief. Well he doesn't promise anything, but I trust my doctor. I'm desperate. And miserable. And in agony.

Every three months, I sit in the same office. He orders the same blood tests. My levels do not change. My symptoms do not change. I do not sleep or eat or love or hate. I exist. I go through the motions. I bide my time. For what?

The demons use a hint of truth, burning lies into my heart. Their stories, my stories, confirm it. "She can't keep up the fight," Fear adds.

"She knows she deserves it," Regret chimes in.

Thud. Mom's arm collides with my chest, slamming the breath out of me. *Oh, yes. If I could just stop breathing. Please Jesus, let me stop breathing.* Blinding headlights from that fateful morning all those years ago, burn the lava tentacles deep into my soul.

"You deserve your pain. You will never be rid of it. Why do you fight? You know you want to rest. We can give you rest. Just trust us. Give into us. Let go."

Demons of doubt and despair, fear and regret overwhelm.

Burning sand adheres to my moist skin, refusing to release.

Crushing the brake, sharp pain in my right foot jolts me up. My right hand sinks into the fire sand. Rolling over, my left arm falls forward, yanking my shoulder out of socket. I wince as Knife digs his rusty groove. I force myself to my feet and step back out onto the harsh, black asphalt.

Embracing my pain, I lock it back up. I gather the broken pieces of my soul, shoving it all inside, like hastily packed luggage.

Don't look too hard at each of those pieces. Just get going. Get back to the business of surviving life. One piece, blinding headlights. Another, Mom's arm. Stubborn pieces fall out onto the ground, refusing to be packed away. I'm too tired to care. Then the breath, or that moment without breath claws its way out.

My knees fold, crushing against asphalt. Peace folds into my soul remembering when oxygen was not required, the quiet stillness when my body didn't even need my body. The endless moment just after impact.

Mom's neck snapped. My head whipped, severing nerves from the spinal cord. We died, well she did. My diaphragm collapsed, and I stopped breathing.

Is that death? It sure was peaceful.

Just as quickly, breath is forced in. My body is violently returned to life. They peel my griped fingers, extracting me from the car, from my mother, from the quiet stillness and into agony.

No, this piece cannot stay out. I crumple it up, stuffing. Stuffing it deep inside. Put on your flight test engineer hat and get to work.

Safe within normal operating limits.

24
Magnolia Grandiflora

Electricity fires through my arm. My eyes and teeth clench tight. The rest of my body remains lifeless, undisturbed, prone, too exhausted to react. The pain is now so common, my body doesn't even bother to acknowledge it.

Mattie sits next to me, her nose inches from my own. Her soft, deep-brown eyes penetrate my heart. She is a gift, oxygen to my shattered self.

"Get up. It's time for a walk, Mom." She places a paw on the couch. It's not a question. I'm not given a choice.

Tightening my abs, I heave up. I press my arm against my chest, grasping my shirt to keep that dead thing from falling to my side. The leash sits at her feet. Wonder when she got that.

"Okay, baby, but just a short one."

One step out the door, the heat like a sauna penetrates deep into my bones. The speckled black sky descends, enveloping. Her tag, a little, blue bone with "Mattie" engraved on one side and my name and phone number on the other, clinks against the metal clasp at the end of the leash. The agony that is me quiets in the stillness of the Texas summer night.

Shoulders slumped, I take deliberate steps one at a time, flip flops clap with each. Ragged jammie-bottoms brush the pavement. Exercise for my soul, Lil' Mae and I stroll. Well scoot, if I'm honest. My left arm dangles at my side. I can't be bothered with my sling, and then realize I'm not even wearing a bra.

That flaccid arm bangs against my hip, shooting razor-sharp current down from my shoulder, cracking open my humerus and radius bones. Just before it fires out the burning ice cube that was once a thumb, it rests, intensifying, magnifying the fire and the ice.

I ignore it, lacking the energy to even wince. But just in case I missed it, it decides to make a wide circle in the open air, piercing, like an arrow, the same spot right where the scapular acromion and humeral head meet.

I fight. I focus on other senses. Magnolia blossoms and crickets soften the ache. At the first street light, the road begins a gentle incline, and Mattie stops to smell. Looking up. Barely raising my head to see the stop sign, an insurmountable five hundred feet away.

"Maybe we'll just go to the stop sign tonight, okay?" I lean over, gently tapping her shoulder blade.

She exhales, stepping forward. I follow. The razor-sharp, current-filled arrows continue their assault.

I step forward one foot at a time. What more can I do but take the next step? Before I know it, the steps are lighter as someone else joins us. A presence. A gentle presence. A feeling really. Nothing I can see or smell or touch. It's a strength. The stop sign is already behind us.

But I do feel it radiating up the leash. And I do smell the sweet magnolia. And I do hear the buzz of the night. The heat and the buzz and the blossoms enlarge around me, lifting me. Not just engulfing me but invading deep into my bones.

A song begins in my heart. *I love you Lord and I lift my voice...*

Then rings into the night. "...to worship You."

"Oh, my King rejoice, take joy in what you hear."

The presence enfolds my hand, soothing Ice-fire.

"I love you Lord and I lift my voice. Oh, my King rejoice, take joy in what you hear."

A simple song for a weary heart. Mattie steps up the pace, enticed by the delightful fragrance at the base of the next street light. The leash unfurls to the end, and I begin the song anew.

We, the three of us, pause at the light, allowing Mattie her joy.

"Okay, Mae, let's go to the next one and turn around." I give a gentle tug.

She steps off the curb, leading the way.

Just before the next street light, as the road incline increases, we make a sweeping u-turn. Mattie enjoys new odors on the other side of the street. I repeat the song over and over and over. Sometimes out loud, sometimes under my breath, sometimes just inside. Before I know it, we're back through the stop sign and across the street.

Mattie slows, walking just inches from my right thigh. She limps. Almost imperceptibly. But I see it. I know. Her repaired Achilles tendon still bothers her, six months post-surgery. It's her left, like me.

"I'm done, Mom." She looks me in eye.

"I know baby, we're close." I unclip her leash.

She runs ahead, leaving me behind with The Presence. In the quiet stillness of the Texas summer night, the very near presence of Jesus soothes the ache in my heart and hand.

We turn up the driveway. Mattie sits patiently at the front door. She stands as I step up. Tail wagging, mouth slightly open, the tip of her tongue visible. She circles around me, gently tapping my dangling left fingers with her cold, damp nose, coming to a rest on my right.

"Thanks, Mom. That was fun." Leaning heavy against my thigh.

"Yeah, it was. Thanks, baby." We collapse inside, me on the couch, her on the cool flagstone.

My arm tumbles off the couch, yanking at those taxed muscles and nerves. The pain ignites anew. I gather them up, Ice-Fire and Little Guy, cradling them against my heart. I exhale. Exasperated. Wiped out. Spent. Nothing comforts and then I realize he's gone. When did he leave?

"Oh, please Jesus. I need you. Why? Why? Why? I don't know what to do."

Mattie lifts her head, arching her neck. Those amazing eyes. At least she's here. Entranced, my gaze is locked.

I look deep inside her baby browns until Jesus responds. "I'm right here. I never left you."

I sink into the couch. "But..."

Oh, never mind. I don't know what to say or what I need. I just know I need. I really need.

I hurt so deeply. My heart feels as if it's crumbled up meat, charred into charcoaled embers. I ache deep inside my body, but not just inside. My skin, eyelashes and fingernails ache. The grief is complete, all encompassing. Just breathing takes more than I have. I need tooth picks to hold open my eyelids. My ears slump into my shoulders. My chest folds into itself. I don't even have the energy to cry. But if I did, I could not stop.

"...but you do not give me anything." I accuse the Almighty.

Mattie's deep and exaggerated exhale demands my complete and undivided attention. Jesus speaks through the gentle eyes of my constant companion.

"I am right here." She (or is this really Jesus) breaks eye contact, softly relaxing her head to ground. "I am not leaving."

My body mirrors Mattie's, releasing into the couch. I release into the deep, trusting her, trusting Jesus to hold it.

The vulnerable state between eaglet and eagle, the feathers and wing muscles sustain flight yet the fledgling depends on parental care.

As an eagle stirs up its nest,
Hovers over its young,
Spreading out its wings, taking them up,
Carrying them on its pinions,
So the Lord alone led him.
Deuteronomy 32:11 – 12a

Part Three

The Fledgling

This section is difficult.
Listen to your body and
take breaks. I'll be here
when you get back.

25
Visible Grace

I take my seat in the back. Not the back pew but even farther. As far back as I can go. Taking a half step to the right, I consider the cry room with a one-way window into the sanctuary. *Not today.* Like a child, I instruct myself, *you can stay in the sanctuary today.* A chair in the book nook with arm rests to support. I tell myself and others, "It's too painful to sit in the pews." Which is true. My muscles are too weak to hold up my arms. They slump and pull and yank on my shoulders and neck. And my head, it's too heavy for my weak and denervated neck muscles. Years ago, Doctor Kline took some of those nerves for my arm. But truthfully, I need to stay just outside looking in. I don't trust the Church. In my experience, the Church does not have an answer to real suffering.

I'm drawn into the natural rhythm of worship, folding up inside. We stand and sing of God and His glory; we sit and pray for ourselves and the world; we listen to the interpretive exposition of the Word of God; we give our offerings. An ordinary Sunday yet a force churns deep in my gut.

As we rise to sing once more, this force overtakes, replacing me. I disassociate. My standard defense mechanism learned over the years to protect me from the world. "A lump in the throat, a sense of wrong, a homesickness, a love sickness" to quote Frost.

I want to be loved and protected. Grami's voice reverberates with the sense of wrong. "Jesus loves you more." I need His Love to be real. I shake, confused by wrong and right. In the depth of my soul, I shake.

It happens sometimes. A smell or a sound or a taste or an undefinable circumstance can set it off. I strain to force this feeling into the straitjacket of verbal explanation.

I strain for the love of Jesus in an institution steeped in tradition and regulation and dos and don'ts, in an institution that rejected my divorced Mom but accepted her children, making me choose between Mom and Jesus. That's not a choice for anyone let alone a little girl.

I'm dying. My face boils. I need to run. But my eyes are blind, and I forget my legs. My body does not belong to me. It has become disparate pieces floating near me. I don't even feel Ice-fire, and Knife takes a smoke break. Yeah, he smokes. He's that nasty.

Lord Jesus, please help me. I can't do this.

One single thought. One plea to God, ignored.

I'm beaten down to a mess of pain and exhaustion. I echo Job as he feels crushed beyond repair and prefers death. He sees his life as vanity and a burden to all.

"So that I would choose strangling
and death rather than my bones.
I loathe my life; I would not live forever.
Leave me alone, for my days are a breath.
Why have I become a burden to you?" – Job 7: 15-16, 20

I am done. I have no more left. Exhausted beyond hope. I can't do this anymore. This is all so pointless. I am nothing but a burden.

Fighting, straining for relief. Ten years and counting.

A decade of physical and occupational therapy, numerous doctors and surgeries and blood tests and x-rays and MRI's and CT scans, countless supplement and medication combos. Everything fails. Hope fades.

What am I doing wrong? Shouldn't we toil and strive towards godliness? Be good stewards of our bodies (straining for answers in 1st Timothy)?

Oh God, where is Your comfort? Comfort in Your Word leaves me wanting. Comfort in Your Church fails. I trust and love You. I long to be in Your presence, knowing at that time all pain and sorrow will be no more. But what about now? How do I dwell in Your presence now, take joy in Your comfort now, live a life with Your strength now? How? What does that look like? I am so weak.

And that is the point. I am weak, but You are strong. I can't do it, but You can, according to Your Word and Your church. But how? I need practical steps. What am I doing wrong? I don't experience Your joy or comfort or presence.

I'm so confused and angered by Your broken promises.

But he said to me, "My grace is sufficient for you, for my power is made perfect in weakness." Therefore, I will boast all the more gladly of my weaknesses, so that the power of Christ may rest upon me. For the sake of Christ, then, I am content with weaknesses, insults, hardships, persecutions, and calamities. For when I am weak, then I am strong. –2 Corinthians 12:9-10

Really? The grace of God is all I need? This nebulous esoteric thing will sustain me? What is this grace? Can you see it, touch it, feel it? If I am to be fully content with my hardships, if I am to boast "gladly" of my weaknesses, then I need to know what is this grace that God supplies. How does He supply it? How do I get it? How do I use it? How does it sustain me? How does this power of Christ rest upon me?

I seek for explanation in the Bible, but the Bible supports the Bible and is just head knowledge. I need more then head knowledge. Deep in my bones where Knife cuts his nasty groove, I need to know the comfort of Christ.

Romans talks of grace as a gift, not based on works, and having the power of a king, reigning and leading mightily to eternal life through Christ. In Acts, Barnabas sees grace when the anguish of persecution spreads the good news of Jesus Christ in Antioch.

How is my suffering spreading the good news of Jesus and why do I care?

My floating disparate self-coalesces. One final hymn followed by announcements. The ground returns to my feet. Ice-fire reminds me he never left.

The day continues in torture and ends with Knife's return.

Mattie curls up at my bedside, and I stuff Little Guy, Knife and Ice-fire deep into the pillow nest. They burn and shoot and ache. I toss and turn and crunch and cry. Sleep eludes.

Lord Jesus, please help me. I can't do this.

My single thought. My one plea is finally answered as the night transforms into a gentle conversation impossible to put into words because it's more than a conversation. It's an experience like those nightly walks with Jesus but more. He surrounds, and He fills, and He is.

Every part of me that is me transforms. I am me without me. I'm inside and outside my body. I have a body without need of it. Held and squeezed and expanded. Floating and free and frozen all at the same time.

And He says to me, "Your life is not your own."

I say. No, I respond. No, I accept. No, I say. "I'm listening." No, that's not right either. Without words, I say. Yes. I don't need to listen or wait for an explanation. I don't question or hide. He doesn't force or even ask permission. Yet I give it, but not really. I just know.

"Your whole life is for this. It will not be wasted. Your tears. Your exhaustion. Your pain. They are not yours either. I hold them. I hurt. I will not waste them."

I trust, completely. Without reservation. It's a dance, but not what we think of as a dance, where the two are separate. We are one and two at the same time. A line between does not exist. I just let go. But-and more than that. There is nothing to let go of. He doesn't ask me to give up anything. He gives Himself.

A promise from a King to a child in pain. "Your pain will not be wasted."

I drift into comfort I cannot explain. It's not sleep or rest or wake. It just is.

I smell love in the distance. I'm not helpless tumbleweed blown around by the fierceness of this world, nor the powerful master of my life I strive to be. I am fierce and humble, gathered up inside. I am safe and in danger, free and bound all at the same time. Finally, I have a purpose.

I see the perfect, simple complexity of God. He is worthy of my trust.

The contentment and trust I finally have in God the Father are beyond my understanding. I'm leaving something behind but filling up with something at the same time. I don't just know of Him but see His character.

I see God.

I'm not lost, but I'm not found either. He is all powerful, all knowing, compassionate, just, and loving. But the thought of fatherly love terrifies me even from this heavenly father.

His ferocity, justice, and control comfort me. With one word He can quiet the destructive waves. He can banish the demons. He can raise the dead.

He can rescue my broken heart.

Light dances through the bamboo slits, wafting over closed eyelids. The warmth of Mattie's nose softly brushes my cheek, her chin resting on the pillow. Those deep browns wait for me to wake.

My insides shake with thoughts of the promise, overwhelmed by the weight of it, when Ice-fire... Oh Ice-fire, we are not friends. You are not welcome. Knife scrapes a deep groove through my radius, joining up with Ice-fire in my thumb. They dance and skip and nag and nip. I slowly, oh so slowly, roll out of bed, exhausted. And a little bit energized. It's different. A shift, as I hold on to the promise.

So, I wait, in agony and with anticipation, for the promise, for the grace of God to become visible.

26
Into the Abyss

Prescription bottles, the only pain relief option offered to me, continue the long silent march down my kitchen counter. Bedtime, again. My choices don't change, but the combinations do. Mattie's at my side. Her knowing eyes give me strength. Constant, consistent strength.

I take half an Ambien, a Skelaxin and an Oxycodone and return to the couch, waiting for the pain to decrease. Or at least the body to relax. Anything to assure sleep may not be elusive.

With the passing of the clock, the familiar numbing attacks my neurons. Without much fanfare, it ticks past midnight, bringing in the next day. Mattie paws the couch.

I follow her down the hall and roll into bed.

Oh Jesus, help. I'm so exhausted; I don't even want to breathe. The years tick on. The endless plea gushes out of my heart. Night after night it bounces off my rib cage, returning unanswered, shattering my heart.

I still don't expect relief. I ask. I beg. But the plea remains unanswered. I should have chosen a different combination, added more. I still could up my cocktail.

Mattie arches her neck around, looking into my soul. There He is. Jesus at my bedside.

Don't just sit there, do something. You are God. You are powerful and loving. Yet, you are silent.

"And after you have suffered for a little while, the God of all grace… will himself restore, confirm, strengthen and establish you." 1 Peter 5:10

The verse bounces around in my head. Anger rises. 'Suffer for a little while?' Really? Jesus, do you truly understand what it feels like to suffer day after day, year after year with no end in sight? The promise of restoration in this verse is comforting, but the passage seems to imply that decades of suffering is just a little while. Here in my private hell, it's a big while.

The evening drags on. Sleep spurns my plea. Every thirty seconds Knife digs his rusty groove. Invisible flames lick at the ceiling. I toss. I turn. I curl up in a ball. My teeth crunch tight. My forehead presses heavy into my eyes.

I feel my way out to the kitchen and take the other half an Ambien. Collapsing, I curl up in my nest of pillows and blankets and pain. Mattie – or is it Jesus – never leaves my side.

Do something, Jesus. I can't do this.

The pain fires and flames, incessantly nagging. I roll on my left, jamming my hand between the mattress and my hip. The pressure. The warmth. It doesn't help.

Rolling. Pressing. Stuffing. Squeezing.

Ice-fire is relentless. I squeeze tighter. My hand is locked in a solid block of ice. Burning. Relentlessly burning.

Lord, other verses insinuate the light and momentary experience of this life. I know and am thankful for the promise of an amazing and glorious future with my King, but I am suffering now.

Jesus saw a man, an invalid of 38 years, lying beside the road, and knew he had already been there a long time. I guess that's a comfort. Jesus, you see and acknowledge the 'long time' this man suffered.

In anger, legs kick free. Flying limbs entangle.

What about my long time? Do you see my suffering? Do you care?

A straitjacket encases my soul. Let me go. Free me, Jesus. Free me. Little Guy wrenches around, caught in blankets.

I give up and just stop. I release. I give in. I can't move, but Mattie does. She stands, rests her nose inches from mine, and waits. "I'm here."

This is more than pain. It's alive, and it attacks.

She leans in closer. The leathery skin at the tip of her nose touches my cheek.

Too lost to open my eyes, I feel. Just feel her life, and then feel my way to the kitchen, fumbling with pill bottles. My fingers find the little round chalky pill. Methadone. Breaking it in half, one side slips out and tumbles to the back of the counter. The other side, I toss to the back of my throat and swallow with the bit of spit under my tongue.

My arm falls to my side and finds Mattie's soft warm head. She leads me to bed. Plopping. I curl into a heap and recall another story of another man, possessed by demons. *Lord Jesus, you see his suffering as a 'long time'.*

But for how long? How much longer must I endure this torture? I massage the thumb, stretching, squeezing, wrenching it back. For a few precious moments, it helps. I clamp on to my bicep, as Knife leaves a nasty groove in his wake.

Rolling off the side of the bed, my feet slide across Mattie's warm back, finding the ground. Standing in the kitchen, the bottles no longer stand at attention. They are toppled, half without lids. Pills spill out and mix. Turning on the lights, I choose another, but the pain refuses to release. Tense muscles continue to build, as I find my bed once more. I wait exhausted for a change. Any change.

Another trip to the kitchen. Another pill chosen. The bed swallows me. My limbs feel attached and not at the same time. I can't move. Deep inside, muscles feel heavy and mushy.

My heart slows. The beats widen. Yeah, that feels better.

Oops, maybe that was one too many. The beats soften. I sink deeper into an abyss.

Yep, took too many. Probably shouldn't fall asleep. Not that I could anyway. But I might not wake. I really am fading. It's so peaceful. Oh no, that hurt.

Knife cuts deep, as my muscles refuse to give him the satisfaction of even a flinch.

Yep, shouldn't sleep tonight. Ooh, not again, ouch.

Knife digs. My brain barely registers the disturbance.

Not gonna sleep, am I? Oh well, at least my muscles can rest. But really this probably isn't good. Ooh, I need to… Uh, what was I saying? Ah, who cares? Not me. Yep, this is great or maybe not great. Ouch. Yep, not great.

"Hey Mae. I, uh, I need to… um, I'm not sure. So, I need you to… um, ya know. We need to stay awake. Yeah, yeah, yeah. That's it. Awake. K? Okay, thanks baby. Night. Oops, I mean not night. Okay, gonna just lie here and you there. Yeah, there we go. Now we got it."

Pause & Breathe

Scan your body.

Place your left hand on your abdomen and your right on your chest. With each breath, can you feel the energy flow between the two?

We are in relationship to ourselves, to others and to God. We now understand how our inner experience effects our bodies and our relationships.

Our bodies hold our stress and pain if we are not honest with ourselves, with those closest to us or with God.

God. Jesus. Holy Spirit.

What is the first thing that comes to mind? Where do you feel it in your body? No judgements. No edits. Say it. Give it a voice.

Let go of all preconceptions.

God can handle your deepest, darkest thoughts. He wants to. That is Love.

He is already here.

With you.

In the mud.

Flying Lesson.
Be honest with God.

27
Not Just Surviving

Returning from a delightful evening with precious friends, but I am incredibly lonely. Stepping out of my car, the wave rushes over, pulling me under the whitecaps.

The crisp night seeps into my bones, heightening, inflaming my agony. I'm so tired; I don't even want to breathe. Ice-fire slithers out his forked tongue.

Help, someone help. Darkness descends and engulfs with its oppressive weight. Alone in my cold, dark garage.

Overcome by fear, my muscles tense. Little Guy convulses. My heart is going to explode. I'm sure of it. I can't do this anymore. This thing called life. I need someone, something. I need, clawing my way to my house. The distance seems to lengthen with each step. Stretching out, I turn the handle and disintegrate over the threshold into Mattie's embrace. Her chest moves up and down. Sliding my left hand down between her chest and front leg, her warmth soothes my burning hand. I rest my cheek against her chest.

Breathe. Breathe. I can't breathe. Oh, it's not helping. Slow down, Gala, slow down. Your heart is supposed to start to beat like hers. I can't. Oh, I can't!

Not this time. I can't stop it. My heart beats outside my body. Jumping to my feet, Mattie leans against my thigh.

"It's okay, Mom. I'm right here."

What happened? Where did this fear come from? Maybe a walk. Jesus usually meets me on these walks. Bundling up in my black, North Face, fleece jacket and thick gloves, I grab Mattie's leash, and slip the collar around her neck. The cold air bites as the wind whips against my exposed flesh, but I don't feel it. Our usual quiet walk turns into a thundering race. Racing to where? Or from what?

I'm on fire.

"Where are you? Why have you abandoned me?" I cry out to God.

The dreadful void returns silence.

I need you now. How can you expect me to do this without you? How can you expect me to do this, period? How long, O Lord? How long? How many more years, decades must I endure? There's no end in sight.

I need Jesus the rescuer, ready to wade through pain, death and hell itself to find me, grasp my hand, and pull me safely through.

There will be a time very soon, I hope, when I will once again enjoy the casual stroll through the garden where *He speaks, and the sound of His voice is so sweet, the birds hush their singing*. But right now, if I am to *endure hardship... like a good soldier [2 Tim 2:3]*, I need the powerful commander to take charge of my private war. I need Him to fight off these dark spirits of doubt and discouragement. Would the truth of that one thought from my Lord relieve me of all this pain?

Oh, the pain. Angry nerves attack.

Ice-fire consumes my hand. Am I the only one who can see the flames rising high above my head?

Knife cuts through my arm every thirty seconds. He is just as invisible. Except to me.

The ache in my heart is now a fireball. It physically hurts and takes more energy than I can suppress. My blood boils as if in a pressure cooker. The weight on and in my chest relentlessly presses. I can't breathe. I want to heal or at least change. For better or worse. I don't care. Something needs to shift.

It has been my constant companion for more than ten years. I need to see and understand this pain. But there's no visible injury. Sure, my arm is paralyzed but over the years I've gotten enough back, I look fine on the outside. "Why so downcast o my soul?"

Help. Oh, please help.

But amid this "gift" that passed through God's inspecting hand, the command remains, to show forth His praise. It's something I am to accept as *good and perfect*.

Not just accept it. Embrace it.

Knowing somewhere way down deep, in a secret place I cannot fathom, lies my greatest good. Even comfort from the Word of God oppresses.

I yearn to *have the wings of a dove and fly away and be at rest [psalm 55:6]* but am told that this fellowship with my suffering Savior is so much sweeter. Oh, how I long to know that!

Thirty minutes later, I'm home dragging Mattie behind. She flops down just inside the door.

I fizzle into the couch exhausted, angry. Angry with God. It's not supposed to be this way. You say you love me. This doesn't feel like love. You work everything for my good? Really? This is good?

My anger extends to everyone in my life. No one gets it. I need someone to understand. Someone to tell me it's okay to give up, not just okay but understandable and expected.

No one is going to tell me that.

All I hear: You need to endure, to persevere, and to just keep going. Trust that God loves you. That He will give what you need when needed.

But that can't be the answer.

More is required. Life, real life, is not just surviving. But more importantly God must be real. Jesus must be more than nice things we sing about on Sunday mornings or trite things we tell each other when there's nothing else to say.

Looking at my arm, the pain is immense. How can I explain the constant, unending, excruciating torture that radiates down my arm to these people who have no concept of such agony?

After more than a decade in this pain, it is all that I am but not even a part of me. I can step outside it, separate from it. It doesn't consume my thoughts. If it did, would I go insane?

I observe it. I learn to live with it like a guest who's overstayed his welcome. It is not a part of me, but it defines every aspect of my life. I do and don't do because of it.

Someone inside my arm carves a deep groove into my bone, all the way down the arm, shuttering through my body. The other side of the knife slices through the muscles and tendons and veins and sinew until it fires out the tip of the thumb.

Every... thirty... seconds.

But it doesn't exit the thumb. It stays there, makes itself at home and burns. The fire builds, consuming the hand. That hand who has a name and personality of his own. Little Guy hangs off me, weighing me down, sucking life out of my soul.

Ice-fire burns Little Guy. He is frozen into a block of ice that never releases its grip. The torture burns deep into my bones, my soul. Penetrating my heart. The lava flow grows tentacles invading all available space until there is no room for me.

No warmth, no relief. Not even death. Just hell.

But I don't know if that's what it feels like. I've never been cut with a knife all the way to bone through the muscles and tendons and veins and sinew.

The little drawer in front of me is slightly open. I see the glint of the red Swiss Army knife that I bought in Switzerland in 1996. I was there in a small ski village for Christmas vacation with fellow missionaries and friends. We had just spent the last year in Albania telling the people of this former communist country of the saving love of Jesus Christ.

The saving love of Jesus Christ.

"Where are you? Save me. Oh, please love me."

I pull open the drawer and pick up the little red knife, slipping it out of its pleather sleeve. It has a file, a blade and a tiny pair of scissors. Turning it over in my fingers, I open each tool one at a time. Sliding each between my fingers, the cold metal sends shivers up my neck.

I take the blade and poke my forearm, with force. Nothing. I don't feel anything. If I could feel Little Guy, he wouldn't be Little Guy. It would be my arm. I do feel a little pressure deep inside like all I did was poke it with my finger. I move a little farther down. Poke. Still numb. The tip is dull, I reason. Maybe I will be able to feel something if I slide the blade along the skin. It's too dull and doesn't break the skin. Still nothing.

I push harder over and over and over in the same spot. Eventually, the skin starts to mar. But the only thing I feel is that deep pressure. I need to find something sharper. There are other knifes I use to open packages in that same drawer.

I need to touch the pain, but the skin and muscles shelter it, protect it from me. I need to connect the pain of Little Guy to the energy of my arm, to that pressure deep inside. Maybe if I touched the pain, I could stop the torment.

Choosing one that seems to be the sharpest, I scrape the blade against my thumb to confirm. Well I guess I'll give it a try. I gently, purposefully slide the blade down my arm a little less than an inch.

This time little red bubbles rise and roll out onto the skin. The striking numbness shocks me. I dab up the red and look at the shallow slit. It doesn't even come close to touching the pain, as the invisible knife cuts his groove through my bone. My hand jerks, quickly covering the fresh slit. My body jumps into a ball.

I spend a few evenings in exploration, in a deliberate search, in a scientific expedition to the far side of the universe. I make patterns and little flowers in my skin, as if I'm doodling with pen and paper. I don't have wings or even rocket engines for this expedition. I'm forced to search on the surface of my arm. The indifference in my heart echoes the analgesia in my arm.

Only a few centimeters of flesh separate my knife from Knife. When in fact, they live in completely different universes spanning millions of miles. Why am I doing this? How does this improve anything? I'm not healing. I cannot touch the invading lava tentacles, exacerbating my desolation.

I carve two words into my arm.

"Help me." My soul cries out into the void.

A few days later scabs that had formed start to fall off. Tentacles invade as anger builds. These self-imposed wounds are healing, but I'm not. I'm in so much pain. Not just the physical pain of angry nerves torturing me every second of my life.

The pressure cooker in my chest sets off alarms. The deafening whistle blows. Why can't anyone hear it? It's all I see. All I hear. There is no relief. I need to see and understand my pain. I need help.

Is the veiled injury even real? The invisible knife fires through my arm. The lava penetrates into every crevice. I look fine on the outside. "Why so downcast o my soul?"

In anger I take the knife, the sharpest one I have. It's so sharp, I can't see the cut until the red bubbles start to push their way out. I take this knife and a make one fast sharp, deep slash. But this time it is higher up on my bicep. This time I feel it. But I only feel the last millimeter. I cut down and inward finally finding a place on my arm that is innervated.

Angela Kari Gutwein 151

A single sharp sting fires into my brain, jerking the knife away. I watch the red bubbles turn into streams rolling down my arm. Little red tributaries diverge as they encounter folds and creases in the skin.

I felt it. More than the isolated torment, hidden and protected from my touch. Little Guy instantly reintegrated, if only for a moment, with the rest of me.

I feel my arm, and Little Guy disappears for one brief instant.

The sting dissipates, turning my attention from the red lines to my hand. White knuckles strangle the knife.

Each finger releases its grip, and the knife rolls down my fingers, thumping onto the table. Slowly folding a paper towel in fours, I gently put pressure on the wound.

Weeks go by. The scab falls off.

The scar remains.

A visual representation of my pain. Is that all I needed?

The pain. Invisible to all but me.

The pain I do not understand.

You're doing great. Drink some water. Breathe, deeply. Turn the page.

28
Above the Demons

There it is. The fire and the ice explode out my left thumb.

My body. My whole body closes. Clinches. Rolls up inside. My eyes crunch down into my cheeks, and my cheeks fold up into my eyes. I suck in one giant breath, pushing my entire abdomen up behind the ribcage, and hold. All I hear is the deep thump of my heart. I embrace folded knees to my chest. Toes curl. My hands are fists.

There it is. I am pain. All that exists is the pain. Scar tissue grows, binding the pain to my cells. I am deaf and blind. I do not exist. My house could explode around me without my knowledge. The me that is me, deep inside, is simply gone.

Nothing I do helps. Nothing I try changes anything. I need the torture to end. How do I continue like this? Life is endurance, existence. "All things work together for the good of those who love the Lord." The church's answer to suffering reverberates in my broken soul. Are you kidding me? This is God's plan for me? Torture? This is what His Love looks like?

The promise of relief returns a lie.

.   .   .   .   .

"This is new. People are seeing real results with this implant. It's worth a try."

My heart doesn't want to trust, but my body is desperate. I make the appointment. I wait the six months for the first opening in Doctor Jamison's schedule. The nurse calls my name and leads me to the open door at the end of the hall. An entire team is assembled.

Wow, this might be the real thing.

A short, stocky man in a white lab coat is surrounded by two men and one woman in full business attire. The exam table between us is covered in glossy pamphlets and hardware examples. A large poster on the wall displays a happy, carefree family enjoying a day at the beach. The product inset shows the same medical hardware sitting in front of me. In big letters at the bottom, the promise of relief: *Life Gets Better.*

Doctor Jamison introduces himself and the other three. They represent St. Jude Medical and this new and amazing therapy. Oh, wow, will this take away my pain? Free me from this torture? Give me relief?

They pull out the glossy documentation. They explain the theory. I don't hear the word theory. All I hear is freedom from pain. The top of the page reads, "Neurostimulation as a Pain Management Option." I read pain relief.

They will implant small electrodes on my spinal cord along the origin of the pain, where my nerves were avulsed, and tunnel these wires along the spine down to a pacemaker type device implanted just under the skin at my lower back.

"Pain signals travel up the spinal cord to the brain." The woman explains. "The generator, like a pacemaker sends pulses up the wire to nerves along the spinal cord. These pulses block the signals before they reach the brain. The pain is replaced by a more pleasant sensation, a tingling."

I say yes. I give the okay. I put my hope and my trust in this team.

My friends pray. My Church lifts me up to God. First, we ask for insurance to cover this expensive and experimental treatment. We pray for months and praise God. It's covered 100%.

Next, we pray it will work.

The first stage is the trial system.

"We will implant the electrodes along your cervical spinal cord and attach it to an external generator for a two-week trial period," Doctor Jamison explains. "You will need to be awake during the procedure to ensure proper placement of the electrodes."

Awake? What? Not much of a choice. Yes, or remain in agony.

"Umm, okay."

I don't even know what to ask.

. . . . .

"Angela. Angela. It's time to wake up. Angela. You're in the operating room. Can you hear me?"

"Uh... yeah... I'm cold."

I'm naked, face down on a stainless-steel table. A thin sheet is draped over me from the waist down. *I'm naked!* I try to move. I try to run. I try to hide. I'm paralyzed. Beeps and buzzers. Really loud beeps and buzzers get faster.

"It's okay, Angela. You're in the operating room." A nurse squats under the table, her kind eyes investigate mine.

The beeps slow. The buzzer stops.

"Okay, Angela. Are you ready to get started? We need to place the electrodes."

"Okay."

Why am I doing this? Oh, Jesus, please help me.

"I'm going to send one pulse at a time, and you tell me where you feel it. Okay?"

"Alright."

You're going to be okay. Just breathe.

A strange electrical tingling pulses through my left arm. "It tingles."

"That's normal. Can you tell me where?"

Trying to move again, "It's kinda right..."

Oh yeah, I can't point. I need to use my words.

"It's kinda high on my bicep."

"Good, now?"

"Ooh, yeah. That moved down on my bicep."

"Good, let's move to the next one."

"Uh, this is kinda weird." I hear the beeps again. Fear lodges a knot in my throat. My cheeks are on fire.

Calm down, Gala.

"Um, that one was in my forearm, along the bone."

"Good, which bone?"

"Well, this one." Trying to point again. "Uh, I mean the radius."

"Okay, now the last electrode."

Angela Kari Gutwein 155

"Ouch. My hand. Kinda like my thumb and finger and that half of the hand. But it was sharper."

"We have them all placed. We can now fine tune it with the software. I'm going to put you back to sleep now."

"O..."

· · · · ·

Flames explode out of my hand, licking the ceiling.

Sucking in one deep breath, my face crunches tight. I force my eyes open to call Mathew. Mathew is the technical guy behind this new contraption.

"Hey, I can't figure this thing out."

"Okay, what are you trying to do?"

"OUCH! I can't even think or see these stupid buttons. How do I turn it up?"

"There are two big buttons on the top. Push the right one. There's a green arrow on it."

"What are you talking about? There's just a small screen with numbers on the top."

"No, on the top. Flip it towards you."

"Oh, okay." Pushing the button over and over and over until it won't go up any farther.

Awe, that feels better.

I slowly come back to my living room and schedule the surgery for the permanent implant.

· · · · ·

Flames explode. Again. Still. Nothing changes.

But we prayed for this, friends protest. It must work. So, I place the charging paddle over the small generator, buried under the skin and press power. I increase the current to its highest setting. Tingling but also pain. The glossy pamphlet lied. The pain is not replaced by a more pleasant sensation. Both sensations reach my brain.

Mattie rests her head on my foot.

Fire and ice churn inside my bones. Inside my veins. Inside my soul. My body curls and crunches and cries in agony.

Weeks. Months. Years.

Charging paddle stuffed in a closet. The generator dead, but I keep it inside me. A small spark of hope. It could work someday. Besides I can't even process what it would take to have it removed. So, it stays. Scar tissue grows, binding it to my cells.

Methadone. Hydrocodone. And all the rest just numb my soul, not the flames. Abandoned long ago, I keep them organized in the laundry room. I may need them again.

Then I see it. It was there all along.

The pain is alive. It flows through me. It is not me. I watch it churn and boil and crack and flow. Through me.

It explodes and fires out. Then circles back around, violently thrusting itself under my skin.

Weeks. Months. Years.

I fight to live above the demons at home in me.

Pause & Breathe

Scan your body.

How are you doing with these scans? What kind of emotions are you finding? Are they all over the place, or are the same ones continually coming to the surface?

Where in your body? Same consistent places? Does it move? Look at the slightest movement. Maybe it's just a few millimeters.

Rest in that. Let your eye see the tiny shifting. It is not inconsequential. Support that movement. Be not discouraged. Take joy.

Maybe it's too big to grab on to. Can you locate a boundary? Is it cloudy? It may fade into the next. Try to find the core. Does it radiate? Is it sharp? Dull? Heavy? What color is it? How bright or dark is it? What does it smell like? Can you taste it?

Does it ooze through your fingers like Jell-O? You're doing great. Stay with me. Place your hands on your lower abdomen. Take in a deep breath. Feel your core fill with life.

Now see it. Really see the pain. It will not destroy you. You will not fall apart. That is a lie. Say it out loud.

"That is a lie."

The demons shrivel and shrink at your sight.

Flying Lesson.
Feel the pain, no matter how big.

29
Black Angel

Back on the couch, I slip into my evening. Mattie sprawls out on the floor next to me. Her head arches back so her eyes can examine me.

Words without words freely pass between us. She holds the steady search into my soul until she's convinced I'm okay. I let her continue to hold my pain. And I am okay. Well, better than I was. She holds me, strengthens me. Gives me the intangible. The little bit I need to soften and deepen my breath. To stand a little taller.

I press play on the DVR. Just as I'm transported into a world not my own full of someone else's struggle and triumph, Mattie leaps to her feet, and then the doorbell rings.

My body tenses. Nope, not gonna to answer that door. All my energy depleted from a full day at work. If it's someone I know, they would call first. I squeeze my eyes tight and exhale a deep exhausted breath. Yeah, I'm better but not that better.

Mattie returns, sits and paws the couch. "You should answer this time, Mom. I checked. It's good." She inexplicably transfers her abundant life to me.

A swoosh. A burst. A jolt. Straight to my core. She jumps up, makes a giant clockwise circle and plops back into a sit. "Really, this is amazing."

My eyes see more. Colors enliven. My body lightens, deftly rising from the couch.

Through the window stands a young man holding a clipboard.

I look down at Mattie. She returns the gaze. "See, Mom. Good, right?"

Shaking my head, I'm so disappointed. She's always right. "No, honey, he's selling something."

"Look again." She nudges my hand.

I look up, ready to dismiss him and return to the couch. He's tall, but not too tall, and fit. His half-tucked, Tom Petty t-shirt clings to his muscular frame. He smiles. His whole body smiles. His short dreadlocks dance with his smile.

I don't just see it. I feel it. His energy. His presence. His life. Instantly, we connect. We recognize each other.

I open the door with a smile and an openness.

He offers his hand. "Hi, I'm Mackenzie Jacob Prichard."

Our hands clasp. "Nice to meet you. I'm Angela. Would you like to come in?"

"Oh, yes. I would love to. And who is this?"

"Mattie Mae." I gesture to the dining room table.

He pulls out a chair. "She's beautiful."

"Thank you. She's the best thing that's ever happened to me." I slip my left leg underneath, sitting up and forward. I'm mesmerized as the setting sun flutters through my windows, glistening off his deep, dark skin. I need to know everything about Mackenzie Jacob Prichard.

He does not disappoint. The first hour passes, and we've scarcely scratched the surface. Mackenzie is from upstate New York. He's the second of three brothers with a baby sister. He played soccer in high school. His dad works for a newspaper. And he's here in Fort Worth for the summer.

I buy the magazines he's peddling this amazing evening. We choose to donate them to the children's hospital.

What's truly amazing and completely unbelievable, I awaken to desire. I'm attracted to this handsome, black man from upstate New York. And he to me (or so it seems). Hard to believe, but he is just as invested in me.

Another hour is devoured, and we still haven't gotten enough. But he needs to work. He needs to continue up the street. He needs to sell more magazines to my neighbors. We call his boss with my order and move to the front door.

Suddenly, it feels final and complete. An amazing moment with a satisfying end, stretched to fill a lifetime. We don't exchange numbers or even expect to see each other again.

We hug. Yeah, we hug. We really hug, exhaling into each other.

I stand at the open door, watching him walk to the street. Mattie nudges. Her gentle, knowing nudge. "See? I told you."

Life is planted, covered and softly patted down in the soil of my soul.

He turns left. I turn around and close the door behind me.

Standing tall, I smile from deep inside. I'm grounded and secure and full. Maybe I can risk hope. Maybe life is more than survival. Thirty seconds later, the phone rings.

"Hi, Angela. This is Peter, Mackenzie's boss. We spoke a few minutes ago. Is he still there?"

"No, he just left."

"I drove up your street and cannot find him."

"Give me a second. I'll see if I can catch him."

I rush, barefoot, down the driveway and out to the middle of the road, looking left, then right. No Mackenzie. No lit porch lights. No sign of him anywhere.

"I don't understand. He's gone."

"Okay, thanks. Have a pleasant evening."

I return to my home, dumbfounded. Not more than sixty seconds ago, Mackenzie Jacob Prichard stood in this very spot. He came into my life on a flame. We lived a lifetime in two hours. And he disappeared, leaving behind life, hope and desire.

I chuckle, shaking my head. Only God would choose a handsome, black man in Tom Petty and dreads as my Angel.

30
Clear -Cut

Mattie greets me at the door. Tail wagging. Eyes bright and happy. What am I going to do without her?

She came into my life a mere ten years ago. Not even. Her birthday is still a few months away. Will she make it to ten? She can't go potty. She cries every time she tries. At first the vet thinks it's an infection, but that test comes back normal. She refers us to a specialist.

The Lord gave me the courage to give her my heart. He used her in my life to teach me to love and trust again.

Now I feel as if His jealousy is taking her away. Does God take away what I love too much?

We wait in another doctor's office. My life travels around one doctor's office to another. I need rest. How much longer? How much more must I endure? I pace from one corner to the next. A poem hangs in a small gilded frame just inside the door. It's titled simply "Dog." It talks of God creating the earth and the sky, the flowers and the trees. After creating the animals, the fish, the birds and the bees, He walks the breadth of His creation with a small creature at His side.

When they finish, the little creature curls up at His feet exhausted. "What is my name?"

God replies, "I've saved you till the end. You are Dog, my name turned around."

I slump down onto the bench. The room is quiet. Too quiet. Mattie rests her head in my lap. I bend down, snuggling my cheek next to hers. She pushes in closer.

The door opens, and Mattie runs over to greet Doctor Patrelli. Doctor

Patrelli's eyes betray her. I take a deep breath, steeling myself.

She rolls the stool over sitting down in front of me. Mattie slides down between us resting on my feet.

"She has a large mass resting on her urethra." Placing a gentle hand on my knee. "We will need to remove it for her to be able to expel urine. It is very likely cancer in which case she only has a few months."

That familiar knot stops all words.

She hands me a piece of paper keeping a copy for herself. She explains the procedure and cost involved.

The doctor's words jab into my grief bone as acid tears burn down my cheeks taking me back to another time in another doctor's office.

What choice is there? The cost barely registers and wouldn't matter anyway.

Devastating news follows me with equally devastating choices. I am constantly forced to bear up under the immense weight, to just endure. To trust that I have a God who knows the best not a capricious God who takes away what I love.

This is the same God who looked at and saw the righteousness in a man named Job. And allowed his life to be clear-cut. Even after Job's righteous response, *"the Lord gives, the Lord takes, blessed be the name of the Lord"*, God doesn't stop. Isn't that enough? A man is tested and found faithful. Shouldn't God relent? Does He shower blessings upon his faithful servant? No, he allows Satan to torment him even further.

This is a protected life. This is a man loved and protected by an all-powerful, all-loving, all-gracious God. This God knows every aspect of this man's life, even every hair on his head.

.   .   .   .   .

One summer while driving in California, I venture off the main highway and find myself in a protected forest. This is a land protected by the United States of America.

Parking in a small turn-about, I follow a narrow, winding trail. Barely a trail. Maybe it used to be, but now the forest reclaims its own. Birds sing, squirrels scamper and occasionally, the light finds its way through the thick canopy.

Yet as I venture farther in, the sounds change as the canopy thins, ultimately opening to a large clearing. What I find is not a vast meadow with light streaming in from every angle and wildflowers dancing in the breeze. Instead this is a man-made clearing. It's littered with stumps and splintered trees, the ground rutted by large machinery. Someone came in and clear-cut this entire area to make toilet paper or plastic bottles or whatever we humans need.

Is this the kind of clear-cutting God is doing in my life? What is he doing with all my broken pieces?

· · · · ·

I sign the papers.

Kneeling, I cup her now not-so-tiny head in my hands, our foreheads meet. She leans her muzzle against my cheek. Closing my eyes, I breathe in and kiss her. Squeezing her soft floppy ears between my fingers, I leave my baby girl in their hands.

I get to my car but can't remember how to turn it on. Sobs convulse my body. Doctor Patrelli said that this surgery is very complicated, that she could bleed out. They will go deep into her abdomen around nerves and blood vessels.

Will I see her again?

31
Soaked

Tears pour out, soaking my cheeks as I drive down Lackland Boulevard. Salty snot drips between my lips. Choking sobs – I don't even try to stop – heave my chest.

My new puppy feels like a replacement for Mattie. So tiny. So full of life.

Manchester is a miniature Mattie. He could be her son. He tumbles onto the floorboards, squealing with delight. His tiny legs claw at the bucket seat, then he backs up for a running leap.

I manage a smile, slurping saliva-soaked oxygen, as he bonks his head and tumbles once more.

But how? How do I give my heart to this beautiful little creature? How do I rest in his soft warm fur? How do I soak in the innocent joy of a new puppy when just four hours ago...?

.   .   .   .   .

I crawl down 635 in north Dallas. Mattie's curled up in the back seat. This trip, twice a week, is killing me. What choice do I have? I can't lose her. She is my life and if chemo and radiation is the only way, then my choice is already made for me.

The sleepless nights, the fear, the panic. All taking a toll. Not to mention all the vacation hours I'm using, taking a toll on my job. But I just keep going. Keep pushing it.

I ignore it at first. I can't see what it's doing to me. I only see life rushing by.

I'm gasping, groping, gouging for a breath.

Sitting in a parking lot, the last five miles promise to take forever. I glance over my shoulder. Her sleepy eyes, slits, crush my soul. I can't do this anymore. Yet, I must. With my deep exhale, her eyes open wider.

"I know, Mom, I'm tired too." She knows me. I can't give up on her.

The far right lane is moving. I scoot over and exit. One block down, Mattie's ready. She pops up, excited for the next adventure. The waiting room is full of dogs and their owners.

"Hi Mattie." The receptionist greets us.

She arches her nose over the desk in reply.

"You can wait in room three."

"Okay, thanks." I lead Mattie to the right.

We settle into the cold white room. I slump onto the teal Formica bench, unclipping her leash. She rotates counter-clockwise, brushing against my legs, once, twice, sliding down onto my feet.

I need the courage to say no. No more treatments. No more chemo. No more radiation.

Tears well up, dripping onto her head. Grief invades every cell. I taste it. It is my only nourishment. I wipe my cheeks then her head, a wet spot remains. Balling up her floppy warm ears sends tentacles of hot lava, burning the grief deeper.

Two knocks. The door opens. I hastily brush off the tears. And smile. Mattie jumps up faking it just like her mama. Her wagging tail turns my smile real, as Mattie greets the doctor.

"Hi Mattie, I've missed you." Handing her a treat.

"So, we've done a course of chemotherapy and radiation." She looks up at me, still knelt scratching Mattie's ears. "Her films are not showing any shrinkage in the tumor."

Tears flow freely. I suck in a little oxygen. I need courage.

"It's actually moved into her lymph."

I made a plan. I chose to stop. But I can't.

She's silent.

Mattie returns to me. She lifts my dangling left hand with her nose. I brush my hand down her nose, up over her eyes, onto her tear-soaked head.

"I..." The word cracks deep in my esophagus before reaching my vocal cords. Barely audible, it only threatens to break the silence. I clear my throat and try again.

"I... I can't..." Pausing for a moment. "I decided... um, well..." Violently wiping tears, but they refuse to stop. "...I just need to stop."

She's silent.

Mattie leans heavy against my leg.

"I can't put her through this anymore." I'm getting stronger. "I can't do this anymore." No, you can't say that. That makes you sound horrible.

"I mean, this is so hard to keep driving here, and it's so expensive." Take it back. Quick, Gala, take it back. You need her. You can't give up on her.

Looking at the floor, I focus on the lines. The tiles fit snug. Not much of a pattern to follow. I lift my gaze to the exam table. To her hands. Her fingers softly intertwine.

"This is killing me." I whisper and purse my lips together. There. Oh crap, I said it. I can still take it back, right?

The doctor leans forward, deep over the exam table into my personal space, her face just inches away. Her hands, now separate, reach out, gently enfolding my own. She inhales, opening her mouth to speak.

"I completely understand." Her eyes soften and almost glisten with... are those tears?

"Why don't we do this? We'll try another cycle of radiation, no charge, since you're already here."

Why is she doing this to me? I already made my decision.

"We'll do a treatment today. You can leave her here for the weekend so that we can get the whole cycle complete. And pick her up on Monday."

She's changing the plan.

It's okay, Angela. She's just trying to help. But I already decided. I hate people controlling me. What's the right thing to do?

"And it will help us with research so that we can save more dogs."

Looking down, our eyes talk, Mattie gives her approval.

"Um, okay, thank you."

The one-hour drive is quiet, too quiet. The radio blares. The road noise seeps into the car. But the quiet soaks into my soul.

Her absence is palpable. That extra heartbeat is missing. I miss her more than I can stand. Her absence leaves a vacuum, sucking out all the air.

The quiet penetrates deeper, like a sponge, sopping every bit of life out of me. I want, I need, to turn around. Instead...

.   .   .   .   .

I only met him this morning when I was surprised by a wiggly white sheet in the lap of a friend. He wiggled himself free and straight into my heart.

Now, he crawls up my shirt, curls up in the crook of my neck and crushes my soul. His heartbeat links to my own and threatens to inject new life. I'm betraying my little Mae. She's being bombarded with radiation, and I'm finding comfort in another. I'm replacing her.

No, I can't replace her. She is my strength. My life. The only reason I'm able to get out of bed every morning, exhausted beyond words.

The guilt intensifies as he snuggles in deeper. All he wants is love. All I need is love.

But... tears soak his black fluff.

.   .   .   .   .

Memories from ten years ago flood in as this new little guy tries to jump out onto the garage floor. Like before, I intertwine my fingers with his front legs, scoop him up and place him at my feet.

Frozen with guilt or grief or both, I watch him scamper about. My lacerated heart hemorrhages. The pressure in my chest suffocates. Bringing home a new puppy brought me joy last time. Oh, little Mae, I love you so.

Manchester jumps up my legs, snapping me back. I crease my face tight and shake my head, taking one single deep breath.

"Okay, lil' guy, now what?" Extracting a forced smile.

I slowly lift my foot. He slides to the ground and jumps on the other leg. One step at a time, we make our way to the back door. Manchester weaving in and out and between my legs the whole way. This is not my brave independent Mattie Mae. He needs me more than her.

He claws himself up the first step, frantically scratching with his back legs.

"Good job, buddy."

At the sound of my voice, he twirls around and topples back down the step. Frazzled, he jumps up, shakes it off and scratches back up. He runs across the landing and tries to climb the next step, but it's a little taller. Frantic little legs motor like a boat propeller, in vain. I lean down, giving him a slight nudge, and he's off across the stoop and into the yard.

The crushing burden on my heart lightens.

He jumps and leaps and skips and then collapses, exhausted, at my feet.

I am beginning to allow my heart to love another. An ephemeral breeze swirls through the feathers in my wings. I am imagining a future.

The tension in my face softens, shoulders relax.

Bending down, I slide my thumbs – both of them – under his front legs, lifting him to my eyes. "Hi, peanut." I can use both hands this time. Shocked, tears well up. My arm did that on its own. My brain said, "pick up your puppy," and my arms (both of them) obeyed. Wow. I shake my head, exhaling. My face creases into a smile. Joy fires deep in my gut, welling into my chest, lava of gratified ecstasy filling my diaphragm.

He leans in, snuggling against my cheek. "Hi, Mom."

"Your sister's at the doctor, but you'll get to meet her in a few days."

· · · · ·

The early morning light falls across my face, patiently waking me. I pull the comforter over my head, curling up for more sleep and then remember my new puppy.

Reluctantly tossing the covers aside, I rotate up, pushing my legs out over Mattie. But she's not there. My feet don't slide against her soft warm body. How do I do this without her?

His bark, well it's not much of a bark, turns my attention to the end of the bed. All he got out was some air. Sitting in his kennel, embarrassed, Manchester rubs his nose with his paw. He opens his mouth, licks his lips, and tries again. The bark starts out high-pitched. He licks again, blows through his nose, and barks. A deep confident bark. Then lifts his paw. "Hey, Mom, I need to go potty."

"I know peanut, I'm comin'."

His front legs frantically scratch at the wire mesh as I slide the latch. He pops out, blows around my feet and dashes down the hallway. That same gentle breeze swirls through my soul.

"Man..." What is your name? Man... Manwich... no that's sloppy joes. Oh, I can't remember. "Hey, you, wait a sec."

Already halfway down the hall, he twirls around, slamming into the wall; Manchester jumps up, shakes and continues.

Speeding up, I grab him before he has a chance to lift his leg.

"No, we don't do that in here." I rush out the door and place him in the grass. "Go potty."

He sits, looks at me and jumps up, running off. Sniffing around for a few minutes, my lil' boy finds the perfect spot.

. . . . .

A jasmine-scented breeze floats through the open windows. Washed in the late afternoon light, Man-Manwich-Manchester sleeps on my chest. I love this little guy. I miss my girl. I can't give my heart to another, but he's so special.

I pull him up, burying my face in his warm belly. Pushing away, he runs straight over to my shoes. His favorite toy.

"Man... no... what is your name... Manwich. No."

Oh, I've got to find another name. Manchester is not working. And Manwich will never do.

I like Jackson, but that's too popular right now. Anything starting with the letter Z is certainly not popular.

Mom named her dog Zeek. I can't do that, but another Z name would be perfect.

Google search: Boy Names Starting with Z.

Zachary, Zane, Zander, Zoltan, Zacchaeus, Zenith, Zepplin, Zephyr, Zeus, Ziggy, Zlotnik.

Ooh, yeah... some weird names... I like that.

"Hey Zander." He rolls his eyes up to look at me. "Zand. Zandy. No that doesn't sound right. You need a strong name, don't you lil' peanut? Ziggy? Zig." No, that makes me think of Zig Ziglar.

"Zephyr."

He lifts his head.

"You like that one? Zeph. Zephy. Zephyr."

Google search: Zephyr.

A gentle west wind.

"Hey Zephyr." Yeah, I like that. "You're like a gentle west wind, aren't you buddy? Ooh look at this... the 1939 Lincoln Zephyr... sleek, black, fast... just like you."

"Zephyr." Yes, but not quite.

"Zephyr Jackson." Yep, that's it.

"Your name is Zephyr Jackson." I cup his tiny head. He leans heavily against my left hand. The muscles weaken in seconds. I'm getting stronger, but the weight of his practically weightless head is more than I can manage. Disappointment. Discouragement. Defeat. Threaten my joy. Shifting the weight to my right, "it's okay, Gala. We just need to work on those muscles." But doubt creeps in. We already spent years, a decade of them, working on those muscles.

The zephyr blows in hope. We just need to work on those muscles. The work will work this time. It must.

32
My Girl

Deliberately, Mattie walks past the couch and around the coffee table.

She quietly sits between me and the TV, locking our gaze. Her eyes examine, scrutinize and discern.

Our new puppy, lil' Zephy J, is curled up under my chin.

I scoop up the remote and press the power button. This requires all of me. She wants to talk. A silent conversation. An intimate connection. She knows me better then I know myself.

"It's time, Mom."

"No, I'm not strong enough."

"You are. I'm tired. I need to leave. You'll be okay. You can hold it now."

"But I'm scared."

"That little guy on your chest will show you it's okay to be scared. I've demonstrated how to be strong and independent. To trust your own skin. He will teach you to feel your fears."

With a swoosh, the weight descends.

Diverting her eyes, she ends the conversation. Mattie gets the last word. With much effort, she pushes up on all fours, walks back around the coffee table, past the couch, to her bed.

Collapsing, my little girl doesn't even have the energy to perform her standard paw and rotate three times into the perfect spot. She rolls up her gentle, brown eyes, giving me one last glance before they close for a much-needed nap.

Behind soft tears, I watch her sleep. Please don't leave me. I cuddle Zephy in close. No. The guilt. I can't replace her. But his comfort feels so good. How do I give up on her and give him my heart? He's just a baby and deserves my love, too. The turmoil topples me under the whitecap. My whole body swirls and spits and squeezes. How do I choose?

Zephy licks away my hot tears and lodges himself deep under my jaw. His heartbeat against my neck calms my own. Exhaustion wins. We sleep.

.   .   .   .   .

Mattie gently steps out of the car. Zephy already has me wrapped up in his leash. She gives him a look. "Calm down, boy." Followed by a stern body check.

Christmas dinner at Karen's. Mattie goes everywhere with me. It's a given. And I can't leave my new baby at home. It's Christmas. They are my family.

Yanking his leash out of my hand, the boy barrels through the front door, leaps over the couch and gallops to the kitchen. Of course. I spin forward, lose my balance and crash to the floor. Mattie sniffs my face. "You okay, Mom? That boy's got too much energy."

"I know, honey. Maybe this was a mistake. Let's put him outside."

With one leap, he's down the five steps, somersaulting into the snow. Anxious to bask in the white blanket, Mattie follows one step at a time. At the bottom, her right front paw falls into a hole, planting her face deep into the drift. With a smile, she shakes and sneezes. Memories of her first experience flood in.

At the back door, Mattie, like her ten-week-old self, sniffs the new white stuff covering the ground. The initial cold shock gives way to joy as she leaps and skids and gallops in the crisp, white world surrounding her.

I smile. Oh boy, do I smile.

.   .   .   .   .

Light bends through the bamboo shades, falling across my face. The sleepless night is thankfully over. She's sprawled out on her bed next to mine. I slide my feet down her chest. I love her warmth. She exhales. Her eyes follow me, but she remains motionless. My knees, manifesting my heart, sink to her side.

I plant my face in her fur, breathing her in. I need you, lil' Mae. Please don't leave me. C'mon lil' girl, get up. Go potty. Eat some breakfast. I need you to live. Fight. Don't give up. Fight.

Now.

She barely lifts her head, slowly exhaling.

Gripping my left forearm with my right hand, I stuff it under her chest and wrap my right around her in an embrace. I interlace my fingers to keep the left arm from giving way to gravity, lifting her. She slides her back legs underneath. I place her front paws on the ground, but they buckle. I strengthen my embrace, leading her down the hallway. Twenty feet from the back door, my left arm weakens and falls away. I fortify my right grip, pressing hard against her chest. Softly lowering her to the ground. She sinks deep into the carpet. I lie prone beside her, face to face, nose to nose, eye to eye.

My girl is dying.

Today.

No. Please, no. I need you. I need you. Exhaling from deep in my gut. I need you. I will die. The grief bone lacerates my heart. Red-hot blood gushes, filling my lungs. Gasping for oxygen.

Zephy's high-pitched cries stop my downward spiral. Then he barks, scratching the wire crate. Oh, I can't deal with the puppy right now. Lil' Mae needs me. Or is it the other way around? He has to potty. But he'll jump on her. She can't even move. I don't know what to do. But what choice do I have?

He needs me, too.

Leaning in, I kiss the top of her head. Pausing a few seconds to soak her up, I roll over to my right side. I tuck my left arm against my tummy, brace my core and heave up against my right arm. Those deep, brown eyes empathize and identify with the massive effort.

The boy continues his protest.

"Okay, baby, I'm here."

Pushing open the latch, I try to use my legs to stop his brute force. I let go of the door to reach in and grab him, but he's determined to get to Mattie. Zephyr Jackson slips under my fingers, slithers through my legs and leaps towards Mattie. Inches from her face, he skids to a violent stop. Somehow, in an instant, his empathic instinct overrides the baby, puppy drive. He knows.

Something's wrong. Different. He sniffs her ears. Her eyes. Her mouth. Rotates once. Twice. And curls up under her chin, throwing his head up, on top of her neck.

My precious family.

I join them. Like before. Prone. Three souls huddled together in an intimate moment. My forehead fits perfectly in the notch at the top of her snout. Zephy's soft pads push against my chin. We are one.

"You ready to give it another try, little girl?"

I roll over, heaving myself up while Zephy climbs up and around me. Then I see it. Her leg has doubled in size. I rest my hand on it. Boiling fire.

"Oh honey, what happened? Did you do this yesterday in the snow? No wonder you can't walk."

Shoving my arms around her chest, interlocking my fingers, I lift. Zephy sits, patiently. Wow, what has gotten into this guy? He just knows.

"Good boy."

The youthful, sparkle in his bright, brown eyes does so much, lifting my spirit. But they don't see me like Mattie's.

Not yet.

We make it to the grass. She limps forward and tries to pee, but nothing comes out. Oh, little girl, this really is the end. Quiet tears wet my cheeks. She limps a few more feet, sagging down next to the pond. It's a Texas, winter day, not too hot, not too cold. Damp earth is all that's left of yesterday's snow.

I gather her head in my hands, touching our foreheads. "It's too cold out here. Let's go back inside."

"I don't want to move, Mom."

The boy leaps around the yard. He must be a gazelle. Back in the kitchen, he hops along next me, ready for breakfast. Placing his bowl on the ground, I watch Mattie, through the window, sinking deeper into slumber. The tears continue.

I take a blanket out, tucking it around her. Her eyes. "Thank you, Mommy." My heart might not survive this day.

Will she die out here? Right here, next to the pond?

His breakfast gulped up. He sails by us, leaping over the pond. Looks like this is where we're going to be for a while. I go get a chair and settle in for the long haul.

·　　·　　·　　·　　·

Estella walks through the front door. Her body language is strong, matter of fact. Her eyes are soft. She takes big steps toward me.

Okay, now we need to get down to business. I can't put this off any longer. Living in denial is not an option. She's going to make me face it. To act.

Lifting my phone, "I need to find a vet that's open today." It is the day after Christmas.

Before I click contacts, she closes the gap, embracing me. She squeezes my arms to my side and does not let go. Exhaling, my body sinks into her love. Clunk. The phone hits the floor. The minutes slide by without words. Her embrace softens and releases. She descends, looking Mattie in the eye.

I lean in to hear her whisper. "I will miss you, sweet girl."

We sit together, watching Mattie breathe. Just breathing. It is mesmerizing. Her leg is so swollen. Then I feel the pressure, self-imposed. I'm taking up Estella's time. I need to face this. Mattie is suffering. I stretch out, grabbing my phone.

"So, who should I call? There's Banfield or this place out on 30 by Cherry Lane. I guess we'll just start calling places."

"We also need to call someone to help lift her into the car. I can have my boys come over. Did you call Karen?"

"I texted her, but she hasn't replied."

·　　·　　·　　·　　·

We pull in front of VCA Fort Worth Animal Medical Center. Estella runs inside to get help. Mattie and I get one last moment alone. Her head rests, heavy, in my lap. I massage her soft, warm ears like I've done all her life. The whitecap rumbles up over my head, crushing and gushing my chest. I barely gulp enough oxygen. This is really happening.

Two guys reach in from the opposite door. They pull on her blanket. She throws up her paws.

Her head jerks up, looking at me. "Hey, what's going on?"

I place my hand on her head, then gently fold her legs against her side.

"It's okay, baby. They're going to carry you inside."

She relaxes, trusting me.

Oh man, she's trusting me, and I'm going to have the doctor stop her heart. I can't do this. It's not fair. Oh Jesus, please take this from me.

They continue through the waiting room, back into an exam room. I rush to stay with her.

"Hold on. Someone needs to fill out the paperwork." The lady behind the counter reaches out to grab my arm. Mattie is gone. She's alone with strangers.

I yank the clipboard out of her hand and scribble as fast as I can.

A nurse comes around the corner. "Someone should go back with her so she's not alone."

"I tried, but she stopped me." Pointing behind the counter. I scoop up the clipboard and rush around the corner. The pen flies down the hallway, ricocheting off the far wall and settling in the open doorway.

Relieved to be reunited with my girl, I drop next to her. The clipboard tumbles under a chair. I lift her head and scoot my legs underneath. Exhausted, her eyes remain closed. She is ready.

I am not.

That same nurse pokes her head in. "I can give you a few minutes. Let me know when you want the doctor to come in."

"Okay, I'm not ready."

The door clicks shut, and I'm left with my girl and two friends. All I see is little Mae. I lean over, burying my face in her neck. Her heart beats. Her chest moves up and down. Her breath warms my cheek. Doggy breath. Not her best feature.

Karen's phone incessantly beeps. Turn it off or leave. My baby is dying, right now, in my arms. Just leave or be here.

Suddenly, Mattie lifts her head, opens her eyes and says. "It's okay, Mom. I'm ready. It's time."

A few minutes later, the doctor sits down next to Mattie.

"Her front leg is too swollen to place the IV. I'll need to use her back leg, but it might take longer for the medicine to take effect."

I give the okay and lean back over, placing my hand on her heart. It beats.

Angela Kari Gutwein 177

Nice even beats. The doctor slides the stethoscope up under my hand. I push it away and return my hand to her heart.

The beats slow. Then stop. I adjust my hand, searching for any movement. I press deeper. Then lift my head and push open her eyelids.

The deep, brown eyes remain, but Mattie is gone.

Pause & Breathe

Scan your body.

Loss is experienced. Feel it. Let it permeate the cells of your body. You don't have to deny it or find the good in it. Your experience makes you, you.

All the people and places. Smells and sounds and tastes. All is experienced by your nervous system. It orders and prioritizes everything into memories and stories.

Trauma can distort and confuse. Do you question your ability to see the truth? Don't lose hope. You can bring it into the light.

Your neurons are constantly forming, and reforming based on new and old input. Surround yourself with those who will shine the light, those who will walk alongside. Their nervous system will help regulate and nourish your own.

Take small steps, continually returning to the safety of the nest.

Until you can trust yourself.

It may be awkward and clumsy and dirty at first, but that's okay.

Trust your inner voice. Your words may come out wrong, but if you speak from the heart, the words will not matter. Be vulnerable and be present.

Flying Lesson.
Trust yourself.

But those who trust in the LORD

Will find new strength.

They will soar high on wings like eagles.

They will run and not grow weary.

They will walk and not faint.

Isaiah 40:31

Supported by air and
gravity, an eagle soars
with the prevailing
currents.

Part Four

The Eagle

33
A Blessing?

105 Degrees. Salty sweat drips into my eyes as I rummage around in the dark and dirty back corner of my shed. I know I put the Shop-Vac back here. The heat seeps into bones soothing Ice-fire, my constant companion. Why do I have to be hot and sweaty to be without pain? Ah, there you are. The hose snakes out in a flurry of dust.

The sauna soothes another constant companion. It penetrates my soul and gives me the ability to do. To work with my hands... well one and a half hands anyway. To work in my own backyard, on my own house. My heart heals, just a bit, as my ability increases.

Oh, no... the garage is open. "Zephy? Where are you?"

Straining around the shed, I step down, not even a foot, onto the pavestone. Oh, good there he is. The sun glistens off his black coat. My flip-flop slips down between two pavestones, turning my ankle.

I'm going down.

No... no... no. Not again. I can't break my wrist again, so I try to ball up, but I'm falling too quickly. C'mon Gala, throw out your arms to catch your balance. My brain sends a signal to my arms, but Little Guy reacts too slowly. He doesn't react at all. The wrist pulls back; the rest of the arm remains still.

My left knee slams into the sandstone. My chest crashes onto the Shop-Vac. It flips and rolls out of reach as my arm folds up under my belly, useless. The wind is knocked out of me. At first, I don't feel it but soon all exposed flesh is burning. Last year, I fried an egg on these stones. I place my right hand flat to get up off the boiling stone, folding my legs up underneath me, but I can't put any weight on my right ankle or my left knee.

Back to the ground.

I try a second time; this time with my left hand. I can't feel the heat, but I also don't have enough muscle control to push myself up. Zephy licks my face. I roll over, embracing him and pull up. He holds steady, but my legs refuse to support me.

Back on the ground. Burning. My thighs, my butt, my hands. It's got to be at least 120 degrees.

Helpless. Again.

God, this is so hard. Help me. I need you. How much longer will I be locked in this broken body?

Stop feeling sorry for yourself. Get up. Looking over at the shed, maybe I could pull myself up there. I roll around, shifting body parts exposed to the sizzling sandstone. Minutes later and I'm finally turned around, resting my back against the shed. I pull my right arm back and push up. I lift a few inches, but not enough to get myself over the lip.

My left refuses to help.

The grass. At least it wouldn't burn. Six feet away and farther away from the house. But how? I can't scoot. I've only got one useful limb. Roll?

This is ridiculous. Get up. I take a flip-flop off my right foot and place it under my right hand. C'mon suck it up, girl. Get those legs up underneath you. Now.

Zephyr stands strong against my shoulder. "Thanks, lil' boy."

Sharp pain shoots through my knee, then through my ankle. But I'm on my feet. I drop the flip-flop, quickly slipping it on.

Good job. Now get inside. My head spins. I can't breathe. Slow down. You can't pass out.

Zephy reaches up, touching my hand with his wet nose. "C'mon, Mom, you can do this."

I take the five steps to the garage and reach out to brace myself against the house. Closing my eyes, my arm folds against the weight, and my forehead falls hard to the door frame. My knees want to buckle. Lil' Zephy pushes against my calf. "I gotcha."

Eyes still closed, two more steps into the house. I rest again. Zephy runs past me, turns and sits. "Just a little farther."

I open my eyes just enough to see my phone sitting on the counter. I grab it and place it in that useless appendage hanging from my left shoulder.

Maybe not so useless after all?

I wind my way around the kitchen counter into the living room. The couch. Oh, so close. Gotta let go and walk, scoot the ten feet. I collapse, swinging my right leg high up onto the back of the couch. Zephy curls up on the armrest just above my head. The phone falls to the ground. I exhale and fall asleep.

. . . . .

Zephyr licks my face. He sits next to the couch and reaches up a paw. "Hi baby, how long have I been sleeping."

My foot is asleep, but surprisingly the ankle is not swollen. Wow, maybe I wasn't hurt as badly as I thought, swinging the leg to the ground. I push up to stand. Nope. Sharp pain shoots through both legs and the ankle suddenly swells to twice its size.

Slumping back down, I reach to scoop up my phone. I need help. Again.

"Hi, how ya doing?" Estella answers the phone.

"I fell again. I..." My voice cracks. Tears pour out.

"I'll be right there." Her voice turns urgent.

The couch sucks me in, and I fall asleep.

. . . . .

Zephy's barking startles me awake. "She's here, Mom." In a whirlwind, he runs from the front door back to me, licks my groggy eyes and returns to the door.

I slowly roll over. My whole body aches, but I manage to sit up.

Estella walks around the couch. "So, what happened?" Sitting next to me.

"I wasn't paying attention because I was worried about Zephy getting out and twisted my ankle as I was stepping out of my shed. My knee and ankle really hurt."

"Are they broken?"

"I don't know, let's see if I can walk."

She knows me well enough not to stop me. Instead she stands and gives me a lift to my feet. I take a few steps without much pain. But what does that mean? My pain tolerance is huge.

"Well let's go to urgent care, okay?" She tests the waters. "You have crutches?"

"I do have one crutch, which is all I can use anyway."

I send her to the front bedroom. She returns with that stick that followed me all the way from Indiana. I try, in vain, to keep the memories at bay. The hospital. The funeral.

Thankfully she pulls me out of my head. "C'mon, let me help you back to your room so you can change." I forgot I was still all dirty from working in the yard.

I don't want to change in front of her. I've done that more times than I can remember after the six or seven surgeries in the last ten years. I want to do this myself.

I can do this myself. "Okay, thanks. I'll be right out."

She retreats to the front of the house as Zephy jumps on the bed. I lean over burying my face in his soft warm fur. I breathe deeply and steel myself for the extreme effort I have in front of me. Not just all the energy it's going to take to remove my clothes, wash up and re-dress, but what am I going to do if I did break something?

I take one small task at a time until… I'm ready. I make it down the hall, Zephy right beside me. I look Estella in the eyes, pleading.

"K." A word, not even a word, just a letter, but it's all I can give her.

What am I pleading for? What do I want her to do? What can she do? Pick me up again, I guess. I just want her to take it away. The fatigue. The defeat sets in. Just this morning, I was feeling good about my ability. About my healing. Now, I'm back in the hole. It gets darker and darker until the trap door slams shut.

Lord Jesus, give me wings. I need to rest.

. . . . .

Estella comes around the car.

"I think I'm okay. I can put weight on it." I take a few more crutch aided steps. "And the pain is a little better."

I walk closer to the entrance, hopping gently on my right, then left.

"What do you want to do?"

"The swelling is down too." I look around and motion to Genghis Grill. "Let's eat."

We laugh. "Okay." She shrugs.

The trap door cracks open.

·   ·   ·   ·   ·

The busy nurse barges into the exam room.

"Hi, I'm Nancy. What can I do for you?"

"A few weeks ago, I fell on my knee and twisted my ankle..." I regale the long-convoluted story. "It's not getting better."

"You know that we only treat one area of complaint per visit. Which one is bothering you most, your knee or ankle?" She states matter-of-factly.

"Umm, really? I didn't know that. They both hurt. The side of my foot hurts too. It's red and a little swollen." I'm shocked, feeling helpless and defeated. At the mercy of another health care provider.

That familiar cycle begins anew. Doctors. Tests. Waiting. No change. No answers.

"If you're going to make me choose, it would be my knee." I give in, exasperated.

"Okay, we'll get a few pictures of your knee. The doctor will look, and then he'll be in to discuss it with you." She storms out without waiting for my response. Not that I have anything to say.

I'm ushered from room to room, until I'm returned to where I began. Waiting. Hoping for answers. There's probably nothing wrong. This is a waste of time and money. A knock at the door interrupts my pity party.

"Hi Angela. I'm Doctor Meyers." He rushes past me, slapping the x-rays on the lightbox. "You have a patella contusion. When you landed on your knee, you jammed your kneecap and bruised the cartilage inside your knee. You will need to strengthen the muscles surrounding your knee. I can prescribe some physical therapy."

"Okay." I want to disappear. Allow the defeat to take over. In a momentary twinkle of life, I venture a question. "Your nurse mentioned you could only look at one body part per office visit. But I was wondering if you could tell me if my ankle is just twisted and will heal eventually?"

He lifts my foot and feels around, twisting back and forth. "That seems to be the case. Can you walk on it?"

"Yes, it's just sore." My bravery gains steam. "One last question, if that's okay?"

"Sure."

"When I fell, my foot was caught between flagstones. It scraped the side of my foot. It's still bright red, swollen and painful." I take my sock off to show him.

"Can you put weight on it?" He leans back against the wall, glancing at my foot.

"Yes." I roll my eyes. "But it hurts." The defeat sets in. He's not going to help me.

"If it gets worse, you can come back in."

More money, more time, more energy. That. I. Do. Not. Have.

He sets up four weeks of PT for my knee, and I leave, determined not to return.

The trap door slams tight.

·　·　·　·　·

Two weeks into physical therapy and it's helping my knee. I remember the years of physical and occupational therapy on my arm. I remember what good it did. I remember how I went from an arm just hanging at my side to one that could help with daily activities. Maybe it could help again. Maybe I could get some real use out of this thing pretending to be an arm.

Careful. Hope is dangerous.

I'll just ask. Maybe one of my doctors would write me a prescription. But it can't be any therapist. This needs to be someone special. Someone that doesn't do all the same exercises. Someone that will think outside the box. Someone that will think.

I don't have the energy or emotional strength for another defeat. It must work the first time.

. . . . .

Medical history. Measurements. Baseline. Treatment goals.

Pretty standard therapy appointment so far.

But there's something different about Trish. Her fingertips have eyes. They see. They reach through the skin, touching the pain before I find the words to explain the years of torture.

Lying me down on a treatment table, she cocks her head to the right and looks, through her fingers, past the skin, the fat, the muscle to the nerve.

"Right there?" She only half asks almost under her breath.

"Whoa, yeah..." The pain jerks my body then settles into her touch.

I trust her.

She cradles my arm in both hands and lifts it off the table, straight up and then down towards my head. She stops ten inches from the table. Trish cocks her head again, applying pressure. She manages to get another half-inch or so, but my shoulder pops off the table, and I pull away in pain.

Starting again with the arm straight up, she tries another angle. Her fingers looking where her eyes cannot see. She finishes the full range-of-motion exercises, walking through each angle.

"You have limited range-of-motion, but that's from disuse. We'll have to slowly work on that. Sit up, and let's see what you can do. It's hard to tell what connections you have." Her forehead furrows.

She's thinking. She wants to help me.

She rolls a table over and sits down next to me, placing a towel between her arm and the table.

"I want you to push the towel out and pull it back without using your body. Just use your shoulder." She demonstrates.

Are you crazy? Tense muscles pull my body inward. I want to run. I can't do that. I haven't been able to do that for fourteen years.

"Umm, okay. But you know I can't do that." A knot forms in my chest. I hate it. I can't do a basic task. I could do it if the result mattered more than the process. I've learned so many ways to get things done. If I could just do it with my body and continue to ignore those paralyzed muscles.

"Well, let's just give it a try. We need to start somewhere." She places a gentle hand on my knee, dispersing the swarm.

I grab my wrist with my right hand and place it on the table.

"Wait a second." She pauses and looks at me. "Do you need to do that?"

"Do what?" Confused. I haven't done anything yet.

"Do you need to place your arm or is it habit?"

"Well, I don't know." I place it back in my lap and start over.

Looking at my arm, I tell it to move. The top of my shoulder lifts towards my ear, then the bicep jerks slightly, finally followed by the wrist as I clench my fist together. I throw it forward, letting it crash to the table.

"It's there." I smirk, rolling my eyes at myself. Disgusted at the clumsy display.

I slump forward, wanting to grab my arm and tuck it in against my chest, but leave it lifeless on the table.

"It's okay, we'll figure it out step-by-step. There's a lot of muscles that need to fire in unison to get your arm on the table. Try to push it out using your scapula." She places both her hands on my shoulder, stabilizing it from the front and the back.

"Can you feel that?" Stretching her fingers under my scapula, they press hard into my back.

"Yes, kind of. It's more of a deep pressure. I don't feel the surface." I shake my head, trying to push out the toxic thoughts.

How do I move muscles I can't feel? This body will never work right. Why even try?

"Use that muscle to push the arm forward." Her words yank me back to the exam room.

Sitting up straight, I focus with every ounce of brain power. Fire. Muscle. Fire. I feel a deep sensation in my brain. I pick a neuron to send the signal to my scapula. Fire. Move that muscle. The one Trish is touching.

A single strand of silk floats in, melting neurons together. Her touch completes the link between my brain and the muscle.

The arm jerks forward.

Wow. I breathe deep all the way to the bottom of my diaphragm. Pure and unrestricted. Wow.

In disbelief, a tsunami rushes in. Happiness – I think this is what happiness feels like – wells up in my chest, relaxing my furrowed brow, forcing my cheeks to curl into a smile.

"I did it." Rotating to look Trish in the eyes.

Tears. Really? She's crying.

"How did I do that?" And the adventure begins.

"Looks like we have something to work with." Her tears turn into a profound, bottomless smile.

We embrace. My heart sinks, a little, as my left doesn't participate.

"I have more than I thought I did. I just needed someone to show me. All because I fell. I wouldn't be back in therapy if I hadn't."

Another setback turns into a blessing. Hope in my soul ignites anew. Cautiously. Tentatively. It ignites.

34
Promise of Relief

Doctor Harris leaves the room. Can I do this again? Trust another doctor. Put my hope, my heart, on the line once more.

Fifteen years, two months, twenty-six days, three hours and thirteen minutes.

Is it time to accept the pain and get to the business of life? Oh, but I'm so frustrated with the vanity of it all.

My search for a cause has returned vain. My fight to keep the demons at bay, just as vain. The comfort I hear from the Church and the Bible instructs perseverance. Look to the God of all Comfort, and He will give you the desires of your heart. He has a plan for you. This too is for your good.

Two broken bones. Chronically acute pain and exhaustion. Post-Traumatic Stress Disorder. A soul on fire. And a paralyzed arm.

Five surgeries. Four occupational therapists. Five physical therapists. A neuromuscular massage therapist. Two acupuncture therapists. Thyroid, hormone, cortisol and iron therapy. Over thirty pain management medications. More doctors then I care to count or remember.

Yet I am not able to give up. There is a strength. No, I would not call it strength. It is stubborn determination learned from my mother. A single mother of four small children. My mother fought her whole life for my life.

So, I fight.

I search. I question. I wrestle with God.

Doctor Harris seems different. For three hours he listens and looks, he tests and touches.

My three-hole-punched story once organized in a red, Presstex binder is now summarized into a four-page document. He reads it and asks questions.

I give him my whole story. I tell him my every complaint. I detail where each pain is felt.

I tell him about Ice-fire and Knife. He hears about my right arm, shoulder and ribs. That pain locked between my ribs and scapula firing up my neck, behind my ear and out my eye.

But I hold back. I padlock the door and post the guard dogs. I recite my story with facts, giving my physical pain. He's a doctor. What does he know of the soul?

After three hours, he leaves me alone with my thoughts. Hope begins again. I'm pretty sure he just told me, "I can take that pain away."

It's called neural therapy. It works to normalize function of the autonomic nervous system by injecting local anesthetics into scars, autonomic ganglia (clusters of nerves), trigger points, acupuncture points, sites of trauma, glands and other tissues.

Scars. Trauma sites. Oh crap, I have lots of those. I muster the fight. I gather bones and muscles. I tighten my core and do it. Once more, I do it. Creased forehead. Locked jaw. I do it.

I schedule six-to-eight treatments. "On average, it takes six-to-eight treatments to see results."

He says.

.   .   .   .   .

Two weeks. I wait two weeks for the first treatment. Now, one hour into the first treatment, on an exam table in a room more closely resembling a living room than a doctor's office, we test scars and trauma sites. We start at one end of my body, moving systematically.

Soft afternoon light dapples through the open shades. In the courtyard, water launches into the air and cascades down the fountain, as Doctor Harris moves to the scar. You know, the scar. The scar that started it all. That rugged road slicing down my neck, across the front of my shoulder and rooting deep inside my armpit.

Piercing the tip of the scar, he burrows the length of the two-inch needle, injecting Procaine as it's removed. The cold liquid squirts my cheek. He repeats the process along the entire length of the scar.

"I'm completely dizzy. My body doesn't feel good. Kind of nauseous and super nervous."

A sharp pain shoots through my head behind my eyes, forcing them closed.

"The back of my head feels like a rock. It's so heavy. My lips are numb." My teeth start to chatter. "I have cotton mouth, and my throat feels swollen. It's getting hard to breathe."

"Just let go. You're reliving your surgery."

Run. I need to run. I shake my arms above my body, both of them, at the same time. Holy cow! Both of them at the same time. Bees swarm in my brain.

• • • • •

Ten years ago, honeybees moved into the rotted out underhang behind my home. I know repair is required, and hive removal needed, but I can barely take care of myself. Purchased food for printed out recipes sits in the fridge until its life ends, not in my stomach, but as dried-up black clumps in the trash.

I am like the Israelites of the Old Testament aimlessly wandering through the wilderness, their only sustenance, white flakes left by God for them to gather each morning. Mine is similar. Every morning, my gathered grief sits in my gut. Twizzlers fill my stomach, while Whitney's weekly dinner invite gives me more than sustenance.

For years, I live in harmony with my honey bees. The hive soon grows to over 500,000 strong. Until one summer day, I notice a large, buzzing mass covering the rotted opening. I dismiss it, pushing the mower down the hill within a foot or two of what I'm sure is my hive.

A few wayward bees come down, as usual, to greet me. But these bees are aggressive, flying around my head. The first sting shocks the mower from my grip. The next ten send me flying to the opposite side of the yard.

The attack follows, gaining strength. Zephy jumps and leaps and yelps, gulping down the nefarious herd one at a time. They are down my shirt, in my hair and covering my face. I eventually learn my bees are under attack from an Africanized hive.

Escape, impossible. My only thought, run. All I feel, pain. Eyesight, obscured. All my senses hone to a singular task.

• • • • •

This attack is not from without. I can't fight it or run from it or hide from it.

The insidious assault is from within. Everything is so fast and loud and bright.

My heart and lungs move on opposing frequencies. It feels as if this incongruence is sure to break me into a thousand pieces.

Eyesight, obscured. My brain is blind. All my senses disappear save one... fear. It's too fast or too loud or too hard. I press my hand against the side of my head, shaking it.

He places his hand on my shoulder. It's so soft, I barely feel it, but the energy instantly dissipates into his touch. I thought this was going to be body work, not soul work.

My eyes slowly open, then focus on a ceiling tile. I follow the line across the ceiling, to the wall, out the window, to the water, then straight to his eyes.

"Don't hold anything back."

Are you kidding me? If I open the flood gates... well, you don't want me to open the flood gates. Can't we just focus on the physical pain?

•

35
Between Fear and Freedom

A whisper thin layer of fresh snow blows along the top three inches of flat Indiana farmland.

I have driven 380 thousands of times at all hours of the day and night and in all types of weather. It's so familiar, I could drive it blindfolded. A fifteen-mile straight line interrupted at the halfway mark by a lone stop sign. Frozen, rutted soil sails by. Thousands of corn stalks impale the ground surrounding us, cut down in the harvest three months ago.

The melancholy oatmeal exchange continues. She knows when I'm ready for the next bite before I do. Words without words.

Five hundred feet away, a quiet intersection with a lonely, red, octagon prompts me to slow. Mom leans forward placing the empty bowl on the floorboard. The clanking spoon makes one last utterance as it pops out of the bowl, settling on the floorboard. She glances up, then flies back colliding against her chair.

Our eyes meet as she flings her arm, against my chest. Besieged by blinding light.

Fear. Raw fear. In her eyes.

· · · · ·

Sixteen years later.

"I can't look." I cover the right side of my face and hold my stomach just under the rib cage. My fist digs into what's called the celiac plexus, a complex network of interconnecting nerve fibers located in the abdomen. It's where we refer to being punched in the gut.

I call it the grief bone.

"You are safe. You're not alone in that car with you mother. You are sitting in my office." Michelle tries to pull me back to reality.

I hold my breath, squeezing my eyes tighter. Falling deeper down the rabbit hole, her voice is fading.

"What will make you feel safe enough to open your eyes?" She continues. "How about Zephy?"

Zephy. Ah. Just his name calms my soul. Memories of his soft warm ears soothe my grief bone. Just imagining his heartbeat slows my own. Yes, Zephy can sit between us and look for me. I trust his eyes.

Sniffing my eyes, his wet nose nudges my cheek. "It's okay, Mom. You can look."

But I can't.

.　　.　　.　　.　　.

Four hours later.

The inside of my chest burns, crushing my lungs. I'm not okay. I don't even pretend anymore. The lie no longer works.

With my back pressed up against the bathroom wall, I stand over the vent. The warmth blows up my pant legs and seeps into my bones. The comfort this provided once upon a time is now elusive.

Curled up in the bathtub. Shaking. Crying. Lost.

Zephy paws the porcelain. "It's okay, Mom. I'm right here." He rotates counterclockwise, folding down to the plush, blue, bathroom rug. He watches. He waits. Then his sharp whine snakes down the rabbit hole, grabs me by the hand and pulls me out of the tub.

.　　.　　.　　.　　.

One week later.

Mom's arm smashes against my chest.

The fear in her eyes pulverizes my celiac plexus. I slap my eyes shut, hands fly back over my face and grief bone. I can't face that fear.

"You are not alone. I am here." Michelle's fading voice attempts reassurance.

A car slams into my mother, thrusting me towards her.

On the couch, safe in Michelle's office, my body folds over to the right. I stop. Freeze. Right here, I freeze. Bent over my right side, I refuse to continue to the inevitable conclusion.

If I stay here all crunched up, Mom is still alive, and my arm is not paralyzed. I realize for the first time I have believed that for the last sixteen years. The incessant pain starting at the grief bone, snaking up through my liver, around the edge of my scapula, through my neck, up behind my ear and shooting out my right eye, is proof I've locked that lie deep inside.

I need the lie to keep my mother alive.

But I also need to live. I want to live. To be free. To fly.

So, I risk it. I take one small step deeper into the rabbit hole, using a neural therapy lesson. The body holds trauma until we are ready to face it.

I risk a slow deliberate motion, my body sways to the left. I test the waters. Leaning against a pillow, I exhale. Sinking deeper, but I cannot rest. Fear paralyzes me. Paralyzes me in that microsecond before my life changed.

. . . . .

Four hours later.

Gripped in fear once again, I rush past sleeping Zephy and hurl myself into the tub.

Curled up. Shaking. Crying. Lost.

My eyes open. The sun has set. I pull myself up out of the tub and spoon up with Zephy.

. . . . .

Twenty-four hours later.

Zephy and I hurl ourselves into the tub.

Curled up. Shaking. Crying.

Not lost.

Zephy stands over me, holding guard, keeping me grounded.

. . . . .

One week later.

The fear in her eyes pulverizes my celiac plexus.

"You are not alone. I am here." Michelle's fading voice attempts reassurance.

A car slams into my mother, thrusting me towards her.

Swooshing. Cracking. Scratching. Crunching. Roaring, deafening sounds like thunder in my soul.

Newton's opposite and equal, force us to the left. The crack of her neck reverberates throughout my whole body. My head splinters the window. The car spins and comes to a rest in the center of an icy, isolated intersection. Thousands of corn stalks impale the ground surrounding us, cut down in the harvest three months ago.

Mom's head rests on my knee. I'm slumped over her. The car is broken and mangled and shattered around us. I cannot move. My left arm is internally rotated and tucked at my side between the seat and the door. It refuses to move. It must be stuck. Confined. Bound. I place my right hand on Mom's face. I want to lift her head but need my other hand. It still refuses to move. "Mom. Mom. Are you okay? Wake up."

Safe on Michelle's cushy, warm couch, I'm freezing. My arm is paralyzed again. Grabbing the wrist, I lift it straight up and release. It slumps internally rotated, tucked at my side between my thigh and the couch. Restrained. Imprisoned.

Shaking. My body shakes uncontrollably.

"Just let your body do what it wants to do." Her voice floats in from another world.

I start to extend my right hand to place it on my invisible mother's face, but yank it back, squeezing my fist. Fingernails dig in. I'm lost in that space between the icy intersection and Michelle's white, leather couch, between fear and freedom. Which is real? What do I latch on to?

Back in my frigid Subaru, I want her face next to mine. Shattered glass all around. My arm won't move. I can't lift her head. Is she gone? Is she breathing? She's facing the dashboard, well what's left of it. I can't see her eyes.

But I feel her absence.

No. Please, Mommy, I need you. Where are you?

I lean over to get as close to her as possible. Ignoring the sharp pain shooting through my right ribcage, I need to feel her life, to breathe her in, to just be with her.

"You were alone then. You are not anymore. You are right here." Michelle's voice is too far away.

Straining closer, her cheek brushes mine. Well kind of. I can't get close enough. The little hairs on my cheek strain. Everything fades away. It's quiet, peaceful. Just the two of us.

Closing my eyes, I breathe it out. My life. I breathe it out and rest. Rest. With my mommy.

I let go.

We are in the car and not at the same time. Well it's just me. Mom is gone and so is the weight of this world. Empty. I am completely empty. There are no regrets. No fears. No burdens. But I'm also filled to overflowing. I need nothing. I have no desires. No hopes. No dreams. I need nothing. I don't even need my mother.

I am free.

Screaming sirens. Men surround the car, pulling us apart, drowning me in fear. The burdens are overwhelming. In my mind, I claw on to her, to anything. I can't distinguish reality. I'm pretty sure I can't move. She slips through white knuckles. The grief bone punches through my chest, lacerating my lungs, as I strain to return. Boiling blood gushes, choking and crushing and suffocating my heart.

They pull me. They push me. They force me to breathe. Agony rushes in. The pain is paralyzing. They strap me down. Paralyzed. Bound. Restrained. Manacled. Locked up.

I give in and give up. I crawl deep inside, finding refuge in the dark, warm recesses.

I am frozen in that moment. Lost between fear and freedom.

"You are in control. You don't have to leave her." Michelle's distant voice beckons.

I return and rest. I gather her head to mine. I bury my face in her neck. I squish our cheeks together. I breathe her in.

I have my mommy.

"Can I come back? Will she be here if I leave?"

"Yes, you are in control."

"Okay." My heart slows.

"Can I come back? I like to come back."

"Yes."

"Okay." But she might disappear if I open my eyes.

"Can I look? Is it okay to open my eyes?"

"Yes."

"Okay. But can I come back?"

"Yes."

"Okay." Opening my eyes, I release my fist. The nails leave purple crescent moons.

My left arm shoots towards the ceiling. My wing takes flight. It moves. I move.

Standing, I feel the absence of pain. The pain in my neck disappears. The incessant pain starting at the grief bone, snaking up through my liver, around the edge of my scapula, through my neck, up behind my ear and shooting out my right eye, disappears as I exhale.

.　　.　　.　　.　　.

Four hours later.

The rumble starts deep in my celiac plexus, boiling up through my chest and engulfing my head. Neurons flash hidden memories into muscle fibers. My hand violently shakes.

Please, Mommy, don't leave me.

Choking, gasping through the knot in my throat. Fast, shallow breaths. The lava fires through the base of my skull, up behind my ear and into my eye.

Before I know it, I'm blinded in a full-blown panic. Where's Zephy? Curled up on the loveseat? Fast asleep in his bedroom?

I feel my way around the end of the couch and cross over the six-foot gap. My extended arm finds the loveseat before my shin. Crouching over, I spread my palms along the cool, smooth faux-leather. No Zephy. Reaching out to the door-jam and across the hall, into the bedroom, I fall into the bed. Into Zephy. Soft, warm, calm Zephy. My shaking hand bangs against his jowls. His beautiful, warm, soft, safe jowls.

He just lays there. Calm. Still. Present. For me.

He rolls onto his back, sliding my hand onto his chest. My cheek rests against his. His heartbeat travels up my arm, soothing the fire, slowing my heart. I breathe oxygen through his fur. One deep breath. Then another. My eyes open.

I'm back.

Pulling up, my hands cup his precious head, then lean back down for more kisses and oxygen through soft, warm fur. My muscle fibers tingle. I can't pull away. I will shake if I pull away.

Dishes. Yeah, I can empty the dishwasher. Something to occupy my body and my mind.

Pulling up, my hands cup his precious head, then lean down for soft, warm fur-oxygen. The buzzing in my muscle fibers... if I pull away, I will shake. *Okay, Ang, you can do this.* His little head slips through my fingers as I turn to leave.

With my back to him, I hear and feel him jump to his feet in one swift motion and slide his nose under my arm. The shaking slows as his deep, brown eyes reach into my soul. I lean down for more fur-oxygen.

Jumping down, he walks attached to my leg, to the kitchen. He stops and sits just before the carpet turns to stone. His eyes follow my every move. Ten feet away, he watches. Calm attention. His knowing eyes link us together. I put a plate into the cupboard and look back. Now prone, still watching. Another plate. Sitting, his eyes pull me towards him. I turn. His tail moves faster the closer I get. He can't contain the excitement, standing as I reach him.

I sit next to him. He walks into me. Chest against chest. His chin resting on my shoulder. He breathes. I breathe.

Together.

. . . . .

Six hours later, startled out of a sweaty sleep. Every muscle taut. Frozen straight. My neck, a fallen aspen. Limbs swallowed up in decaying leaves and tangled vines. Paralyzed. Lungs pressed and forced. Vines seal my throat closed.

Roaring, deafening sounds jolt me out of sleep. Swooshing. Cracking. Scratching. Crunching.

Terrified. Curled up. Crunched up. Paralyzed. Bound in a lump of fear.

Frozen in the fire starting at the grief bone, snaking up through my liver, around the edge of my scapula, through my neck, up behind my ear and shooting out my right eye.

The thunder in my soul is real.

Swooshing. Cracking. Scratching. Crunching.

Not real.

Where is the lasting freedom? When will I find my way through the dark and damp? Or is it just a precarious balance between fear and freedom, between frozen and flight?

36
Fire Finds a Home

He shakes. He scratches. He squeaks. Just a peep, really. But I'm up. To my right, the sun peeks through the bamboo and on my left, the orange fluorescent numbers don't surprise me. He's my alarm. I haven't set that thing in 14 years, at least. Mattie taught him well.

Sliding off the bed, the numbers roll over. Six zero zero. He doesn't know it's Sunday, and I don't care. That was a good night. I'm rested and ready to face the day. I might even go to church, but I don't have to worry about that yet. Four hours of perfection await.

I've had a pretty good week this week as weeks go these days. Fairly calm. No surprises or tragedies to speak of, which keeps the PTSD at bay. That pesky fear. Things get so fast and loud and bright. I can't stop it. But not this week.

This week was nice. Work was great. I can succeed there. I'm needed. My voice is heard. PT and OT were pretty good as well. I guess. Trish and Jason hear me. See me. Try to help me. Trish gave me a few new exercises. I've been doing them but just a few times. They don't seem to help much, but I'll keep an open mind, for now.

Yesterday, I spent the whole day at a writing conference. Oh, my book is so close, but I just can't find the ending. I can't wrap it up in a happily-ever-after bow because that's a lie.

I'm exhausted. I'm in pain. Still.

Is that the ending? Is that my message? Learn to live in the pain. With the pain. Is that flying?

Our routine begins with a jaunt around the backyard. He sniffs and moves and sniffs and moves until he finds the perfect spot. Leaping into a sprint, his circuitous search ends with a straight line to the back door, where he turns and sits, tongue drooping off to the left. I'm not the gazelle he pretends to be, so it takes me a little longer to close the distance. Bare feet, wet from the morning dew, leave prints on flagstone.

Bright eyes barely able to contain his excitement greet me. He pops his hind legs up as I step up onto the back stoop. Lil' Zephy circles around, brushing against my legs. He waits behind me, that precious nose resting on my thigh, until my foot crosses the threshold, matching me step for step. His eyes follow my hand to the doorknob. The excitement can no longer be contained, he shoots past me straight to the fridge.

"Food, Mom, food!" Zephy sits, pops up and sits.

"Are you hungry, lil' boy?"

"Yeah, yeah, yeah!" He leaps into the air and back down to a sit. His tongue slurps out and back in.

"Okay, here you go." He jumps up, circling around. Excited eyes follow my every move.

Yep, we've got this routine down. I pull out his bowl and my Trader Joe's coconut creamer and cold brew coffee concentrate just as the electric kettle spouts its magic steam.

I mix up my concoction and place his on the ground. We are quite the pair.

The shiny aluminum bowl reflects his visage. Slurping his chops, he leads me back out. Seventy-five degrees will soon turn to ninety-eight according to my iPhone. I leave that on the kitchen counter. Only my dog and my coffee join me for this perfect moment, igniting my soul. This is where I find God. The sun, slowing rising above my house, licks the stone wall to the west. Zeph laps around the yard, inspecting every inch.

I take my seat. The best seat in the house. Right down front, center stage. The curtains rise. Tap. Tap. Tap. A chorus of crickets, cicadas and katydids echoes against the back wall high up in the balcony.

Water droplets cling to wispy blades of Bermuda and stocky Saint Augustine. Larger droplets cascade down rocks and bounce off lily pads. The orchestra builds with the sharp squeal of squirrels teasing Zephy. Clapping cymbals. He barks and leaps and thinks he can climb. Snare drums swoosh in with a rush of leaves. Boom. Bending branches. The woodwinds fill in with the deep woo of a dove. A soloist stands high atop the wire ready for her grand entrance. She's tiny and does not own a shiny, sequined gown like the rest of the orchestra, but her voice silences the hall.

Zeph returns, reporting "all is well." He slinks under my knees. "A fly." Leaping high into the air, he catches the rude concert guest and spits him out. "Who let him in?"

During intermission, we go inside for a second cup and a peanut butter, salmon biscuit.

Just as the second half crescendos, Knife. That ol' Knife. My dear friend returns. He jabs his tip into my left thumb, right at the base of the metacarpal, and cracks open the bone, jumps across the knuckle, cutting a deep groove through the phalanges.

No, please no. Oh Jesus, please no.

Knife responds over and over and over and over...

My body writhes. Hands become fists.

Trish's new exercises? I mowed the yard last night? But I'm not sore. Oh, I just want a reason, so I can find a solution.

I throw my arms out, jumping to my feet. The imagined Knife cannot be removed. The torturer wielding it does not exist. There is nowhere to place my anger. Except God. God?

"God doesn't give you more then you handle." I hear the Church's comfort. "His grace is sufficient." Sufficient? For what? Grace? This is grace?

Knife digs. My body curls into a ball.

"We know all things work together for good to them that love God..." I don't know that. This doesn't feel like good. My anger boils. Or does that say I don't love God?

Torture. I'm being tortured. Fear and anger and despair and doubt fight to crush me. My stomach growls, but I can't even see. How am I expected to figure out what to eat let alone eat it?

Church is not going to happen today. I pace. The bone cracks open. I crunch up. Knife releases. I pace. I walk from my Zephy to my couch. Back and forth. Knife cuts a groove through the bone. I stop, doubling over. My hand squeezes my hand. Knife releases. I pace. Zephy watches. His deep brown eyes follow. They reach into my soul and comfort. He squeaks. A cry. Concern. Doggy concern. His presence focuses me. He slows the spinning. I rest in the deep brown silence for a few seconds of relief. Until another groove cuts open my thumb.

The spinning room forces my eyes shut, grabbing my hand with my hand. Squeezing tighter and tighter, I fall to the ground and bury my face into his fur. The world falls away as my body braces for the next fiery bolt of lightning to be released. I push deeper into the warmth of his black fluff. The pain engulfs and releases, engulfs and releases, engulfs and releases.

I jump to my feet. Zephy follows suit. This isn't working. Throwing my arms into the air, I take in a deep breath. Yard work? Hot sweaty work helped before. This is not going to end, not today. Probably not tomorrow. Maybe the next. Make a choice. Stay in a ball or get going. Either way, you will be in pain.

"Okay, buddy. Let's go." We run around the kitchen counter, through the garage, over the flagstone and into the grass. The beads of water have all burned off. The sun directly overhead. The sauna seeps into my bones. Heat soothes. Zephyr leaps around the pond, swooshing past me. Around and around, he returns each time. The deep brown beckoning me to join.

I slip on my gloves, grab my poker-sticker, and march to the back-left corner of the yard. A large weed patch is no match for my poker-sticker. Sweat drips into my eyes. Relentless pain engulfs and releases. The weeds pop and crack as I find the roots. Some of the salty droplets roll into my mouth before my muddy gloves wipe them across my cheek. Zephyr finds a shady corner, digs a shallow hole and watches. His eyes investigate mine every time I glance over.

My fingers lose grip, as Knife cuts deep, dropping the poker-sticker into the weed pile. Doubling over, the blood rushes, the heat overwhelms. I stumble to Zephy's corner, collapsing on him.

He shifts and exhales. "Oh, Mommy, I'm so sorry."

I need a poker-sticker to root out this pain.

Returning to the house for some water, we collapse on the floor. I stop. For a few moments, I stop. Knife remains relentless, maybe even worse. I can't stop. I can't look at it. It's too fast. Too loud. Too bright.

"C'mon Zeph, let's mow the front yard. Maybe the vibration will shake out this pain."

He finds another shady corner, digs another shallow hole and watches.

Always watching.

Sweat drips. Torture continues.

"Maybe a hot shower? What do you think?"

"Yeah, yeah. Good idea." He jumps up, and then down into a sit, tongue hanging, eyes bright.

"I could say anything, and you'd be excited."

And that brings me joy. The happiness in my heart starkly contrasts against the deep grief, welling up in the background, I don't have the energy or emotional fortitude to face. Fortunately, the intense physical agony devours my attention.

Nothing works. I pace, this time outside as the sun moves across my yard. After twelve hours of constant torture, I'm ready for bed. I'm going with meds tonight. I squirreled away what's left of my stash. The pain is so intense, I can barely read the bottles. Ooh yeah, I think that's a muscle relaxer. I could use that. My body is so tense. Knife fires as I push and turn. This is why I never put on these lids. It pops off and flies across the room. I break the pill in half. It's been a while since I've taken this stuff. I probably don't need much.

The real stash is in the laundry room, a drawer full of narcotics. The first bottle looks good enough. I think it's an oxy something-or-other. I most certainly don't break that one in half. I want the full effect. My body relaxes, sinking deep into my pillow nest, but the sleep is not deep or constant. I wake. I sleep. I wake. I sleep. My body rests but not my brain.

He shakes. He scratches. He squeaks. Just a peep, really. But I'm up. The orange fluorescent numbers are a welcome change to my sleepless torture. Monday. The routine is different on a Monday. Somehow, he knows. I let him out and get ready. Digging out my compression glove, Knife cuts his nasty groove. Make a choice. Curl up in a ball or get up and face it. Either way you're going to be in pain.

Give up or live?

A different kind of busy takes up the day. The torture continues through its cycle. At hour thirty, Knife cuts less and Ice-fire burns deeper. I welcome Ice-fire. Wow, did I just say that? I'm at a point where I welcome the torture I fight to rid. I spend countless hours and countless dollars to find a cause, to find the source and to find the answer. Now thirty hours under the knife, and I welcome the burn. And it burns deep inside my bone. It moves. It breathes.

It lives inside me. It moves me aside and finds a home.

If I could just dig it out.

Hour thirty-six. I yank off the glove. My hand can breathe, but so can the fire. Bedtime, again. I stuff the fire and hand deep into the pillow nest. No drugs tonight. Nothing can quench the flames. Ice ignites fire.

Shake. Scratch. Squeak.

Another day, another choice.

Pause & Breathe

Scan your body.

Another day, another choice. Life is a choice. No one can make it for you.

What is your true need? To find that, I will invite you to go back to your body. Find your inner experience. Where are you holding? What is the resistance trying to teach you?

Close your eyes and listen.

What is your story? How is it shaped by the people and places surrounding you?

We have looked at our inner experience through many lenses. The darkness cannot crush us. Our bodies protect us. Our pain and our triumphs can be felt. We can be present and honest while staring into the demon.

Our inner voice is trustworthy.

We stumble and crawl and trip and grope. The tears dried up years ago. All that's left is a groan.

It seems, no matter what we do, nothing changes. The pain remains.

Can you be okay with that? Can you release the striving, and trust the process?

Flying Lesson.
Sometimes it doesn't change. That's okay.

37
Patient Persistence

The force ignites anew, folding my gut into knots. The trigger dissolves in stubborn and complicated brain chemistry, lost for the moment. Intricate and needy neurons, in an infinite chain reaction, explode as a fourth of July finale.

My eyes forget to translate the lights and shadows into recognizable shapes. Fingers rub, uncontrolled, against each other. The energy travels, not out the fingertips, but up the arm. Jumping to my feet, I fly to the bedroom. Contrasting brain signals ignite a storm in confused muscles. I need, but what? What do I need? My arm shakes and bounces to expel the whirlwind. Words form a phrase. This time I choose.

"I can't stop. I can't stop. I can't stop. I can't stop."

Pausing, I crunch my face and shake my head. "I can't stop." The phrase, like a salve, pops out without permission. Slower. "I can't stop." The hand jumps to cover lips. Softer in a whisper, through finger barricades. "I can't stop."

Eyes remember as the room takes shape. I return to the couch. To my last known activity. To the trigger. I straighten the crumpled pages and am transported to a shack in the Oregon wilderness. Transported by the pages of a novel to another time and place.

Zephy takes his place, and then I see it. I see it in my constant companion. His chest rises and falls. Mine slows to match. The link is alive. It resonates, a pulsating force where two are one.

For the first time my eyes open. The fireworks give way to a lone spark.

The lessons began years before the accident. Years before I heard her neck crack. Years before her last breath. Years before our resonant bond broke.

Long before my brain could form explicit memories, Grami first said "Jesus loves you more." More than words, more than a memory. It is life. My life. But it is also an impossible truth eclipsed by pain.

As an aerospace engineer, I was especially fascinated by the solar eclipse we experienced just a few months ago. I felt like that wide-eyed little girl, trusting Grami and the love Jesus has for me. I understand the exact geometry and orbital dynamics required to eclipse this big, bright, ball of fire by an object 400 times smaller, and how the sky completely darkens. From our perspective during a total solar eclipse, the light no longer exists.

But how do those orbital dynamics translate to God's love? How do I know of God's love when blinded by fear and pain?

The trigger.

"Oh Mackenzie, you can't see me through your pain." Papa's eyes overflow.

The patient persistence of the great physician began his work with the deep brown eyes of a tiny puppy. Years ago, Mattie pierced my soul and took something. Something very precious. Something I protected and guarded. Surprised. No. Shocked as the sensation shot through my heart. Was it love?

Those eyes penetrated the callused wall. She quietly sat. Our gaze locked. She met me in my intimate hell, leaping in with all four paws. A silent conversation. She knew me better than I knew myself, and she held it. For ten years, she held my pain. My neurons change and mold to her constant presence, modeling loyalty, protection and sacrifice. I learn to stand, first with her strength, then to trust myself.

In another silent conversation, she transfers the job to Zephy. The link, sputtering and threatening to expire, instead changes color. Mattie's yellow and orange and purple strength is replaced by Zephy's blue and green fear. My strength torn out, ripped away again, we huddle in the dark together.

Blinded by fear and pain, the one that "loves you more" disappears. Darkness swells over, I muddle around, blind and deaf, unable to trust my senses. Paralyzed, frozen in flames, I try to close it down once more. Lock out the pain. Don't feel.

But this time, I'm not alone. This time my lil' Zephy teaches me to face my fears. Feel my fears. They do not destroy. The miracle, they strengthen. The sputtering blue and green fluorescence ignites into a beautiful resonance. Together we face our shared fear. We walk together. We cry together. We live together.

Today, our life takes us to the soil once more.

The dark Texas clay is saturated, refusing to give way. I press heavy against the spade and with each scoop, soil adheres to soil until the blade is no longer visible. I scrape the black goop with force, but it just clumps to my shoe. Pansies sit behind my left hip in a plastic six-pack. Six six-packs in a plastic tray. Purple ones. Somewhere deep inside, I find a love for the purple ones. Planting pansies in November is not something you do in Indiana. But I'm not in Indiana.

My ears burn in the brisk fall wind. Losing the fight to sniff back the snot, I wipe my nose with the back of my hand. My knees are numb from the cold, wet sharp soil. Soaked denim is one with my skin.

Sixteen years ago, after my first winter in this house, I planted these same pansies in April. By May, they were burnt up in the scorching summer sun.

Kneeling in this same spot, I still search for my mother. This simple action, turning over soil, is something in my control. I want my mommy. I need her. I cannot stand on my own two feet.

Zephy sits behind me, watching, waiting. Together we step into the deep.

The imagined control transforms into the same old story. Oppression. Fear. The goop binds heavy to my shoes, pulling me into the cold, damp darkness. It climbs up my legs, seeping through my skin, gunking up my veins and arteries, filling my heart and then my soul.

I dug these same holes. But I am not the same person. My arm was buried in a sling, strapped to my chest. My story is changing. Right now, it's changing.

My eye finds the bright, yellow center of my purple pansy. Deep purple (almost black) lines begin in the yellow, piercing out through the delicate ripples. I softly slide a single flower petal between my index finger and thumb. A silky gift to soothe.

We walk through fear together, banishing it one step at a time. Grami was right. My patient, persistent Papa loves me. He loves my questions and my doubts and even my anger. Even as I'm blinded by the eclipse's cyclical return.

Kneeling in the dirt, I turn and see it in the silky ripples of a delicate flower petal and in Zephy's deep brown eyes. Like when the moon's inky disk travels across the sky, revealing Baily's beads, bright rosary-like beads of sunlight. Light always finds a way, streaming through deep valleys along the moon's rugged edge.

My fear begins to die in the dark, damp Texas soil.

Pause & Breathe

Scan your body.

In my garden, the Lanceleaf Coreopsis sits atop its spindly green stalk, dancing in the wind, supported by the earth, fed by the sun.

Movement with support. All of creation moves and breathes. From the orbits of galaxies to the orbits of electrons. We move. We breathe. And we are supported by every other cell and creature and planet and star.

Every action is the result and cause of another. The very neurons in your brain change when in close proximity to another soul. We are not alone. That is a lie.

But we cannot see the light when it is eclipsed by pain. The darkness swallows us whole, leaving us paralyzed by fear. Can you risk looking it straight in the eye?

If we risk movement, the shift... Oh, that tiny shift cannot be ignored as a bright bead of light pops through. Light brings life. And life brings hope. And hope brings love. And love cannot be denied.

Love destroys fear.

Telos. A Greek word meaning the ideal form one was designed to take. We were designed to move and breathe and love.

Movement begins with support and ends in freedom.

Flying Lesson.
Really live, now.

38
One Breath

Sandwiched between a chiropractor and a physical therapist, Temple Road Yoga is my next option. Neural Therapy may not be the answer, but it did show me connections in my body. The work I do with Trish, and the work I do with Michelle cannot remain separate. I need to make a mind-body connection.

Eight weeks ago, I stepped into Temple Road Yoga unsure of what to expect. Afraid to expect anything but needing something.

Today, seventeen years ago, my mother died. The ache is still sharp.

I step through that familiar door, as I've done nearly every day. Angel's deep embrace assures me. She knows, and I let her hold it.

I spread out my mat. I gather the blocks and the bolsters and the blankets and the balls and the straps.

I feel it deep in my grief bone.

Fellow travelers trickle in. Smiles and greetings are exchanged.

Pressing my feet into the mat, I bend into downward facing dog. My hands land flat and strong, even Little Guy. Every muscle engages, energy traveling throughout my entire body, rooting me deep into the earth.

I lower into plank, shifting my weight from right to left. The left side of my body engages more and more muscles. Little Guy holds my weight, soothing my nervous system, softening the ache. I explore my limits as they are not fixed, shifting more and more weight to the left. Rotating my core, my full weight rests on my left hand as my right rises.

A side plank.

Wow. A side plank. And he gives way. I crash to the floor, with a smile. See, limits move. Every day, they move.

I am grounded and secure and full.

Angel enters with her soft, safe presence and begins.

"Today we will begin on our backs. Make sure your ball is nearby."

She takes us through the holds and the moves and the positions. Muscles strengthen, as I learn a new vocabulary. Asana. Prana. Pranayama. Svanasana. Mudra.

The class moves together with one breath. I love this. My body feels and connects and works.

We rest in pigeon pose. Well, it's not actually rest. A lot of muscles must engage and release and stretch to rest in pigeon pose. I work through each one, when fear overwhelms. Run. I need to run. Now.

Leaning up on my elbows, the left shoulder collapses into my ear. Oh, c'mon Little Guy, work! The bees swarm.

Hands fling and fly. I scrunch my face and fall into my hands. I can't breathe.

The class is oblivious. At least, I hope they are. Angel sits beside me, placing her hands on my back and head. I release with a deep exhale. She holds it.

Body work is soul work. Everything is connected.

The flow of electrons through the nervous system links together not only every cell in my body, but also links each of us together.

If we are willing to see.

That hard-won lesson gleaned from twenty-seven pages detailing the experience of my body before, during and after each of the twenty-seven Neural Therapy Treatments.

Doctor Harris is different, but he is not my answer. My complaints remain unchanged. My pain is still my pain. I gave it everything I had. I did the work. And I am left with one priceless lesson.

I see.

I see connections in my body I would never imagine. My solar plexus is directly related to fear. My grief is held by my right sixth rib.

To compensate for my unbalance, I rotated my ribcage counterclockwise, which elevated my right hip. This causes pain in my right foot.

Now on my yoga mat, supported by my friend, I see why I'm terrified when my sixth rib on my right side sends its lava tentacles up the edge of my scapula, through my neck, around my ear and out my eye.

I see the triggers that cause the trauma symptoms.

I don't just see the paralysis, I see that I am paralyzed, that I am disabled.

From the first moment, in the intensive care unit, I denied that fact. I strapped it to my chest and fought to live, suffering in silence.

It is a deafening silence.

My arm is not my arm. Little Guy is weak. He causes me pain and is a constant reminder of what happened that morning seventeen years ago. He is a constant reminder of my guilt.

He screams in the silence. The nerves are constantly shocking and sputtering and sparking. He is on fire and refuses to rest. The weight of his presence demands my attention. Spending years in doctor's offices, surgical suites and physical and occupational therapy, I record his daily experience for these health care professionals, but it's his experience, not mine.

Now as I turn and look at him, a massive ball of energy fills my left chest, my face boils and my eye blurs. Even my body wants to protect me from seeing Little Guy.

· · · · ·

Back in my garden, spring is days away.

I, me, all of me, the deepest part of me, takes it in. All of it. I breathe in life.

Sitting, just sitting, next to my pond, the clear, crisp water washes into my heart. Zephy sits behind me, watching. Squirrels race high up into the trees, scampering out to the very tip of a branch, and hopping over to the next.

A dove lights down onto the giant boulder in the center of my island. Years ago, I placed that boulder with Little Guy stuffed in my jeans pocket.

Two feet away, my dove takes a drink. A thin, orange line traces under his eye, a beautiful contrast to his soft grey, almost blue feathers. Looking up, he finally sees me, and waits a few seconds before flying over to the waterfall.

I sit in this place I built to find my mother.

Years in this place digging in the dark, and I found God. Becoming like Jesus begins in the dark. The harshness of life beats you down. Smaller and smaller until all that's left is a tiny seed of faith buried deep in the cold, damp soil, where the seed breaks open and is no more. The seed dies, as it's only a shell for the life inside. Roots reach for the water below, while something new and surprising reaches up out of death for warm light.

Life begins in the soil.

.   .   .   .   .

Spreading out my mat once more, I fold into downward facing dog, my hands land flat, and pain explodes up through the carpal tunnel of my left hand. No, not another injury. I'm getting stronger, and not just physically. But I can't handle another surgery, another setback.

I turn and look at that arm, my arm. This time, I'm not angry. I'm sad, and I grieve. I grieve my disability.

Angel leads the class back into reclined pigeon.

I rest my chest over my folded my left leg, extending my right straight back. That sixth rib shoots it lava tentacles up my neck, behind my ear and out my eye. The bees threaten. That same story plays in my body.

I want my mommy. I really, really want my mommy.

Hundreds of hours on this mat have taught me to breathe. So, I breathe. And I hear my friends breathe. So, I take in another. Deeper. Softer. Longer.

We breathe.

Then with the next breath, I feel her. It is warm and soft and opens my lungs. Ooh that scent. I know that scent. Feeling her is not enough, I need to see her. So, I raise my head.

And there she is.

She sits cross-legged at the top of my mat. I reach out and externally rotate my left arm. I reach out and externally rotate my left arm. Holy cow! I reach out and externally rotate my left arm!

And my mommy gently places her hand in mine, and she smiles.

She smiles at me.

Pause & Breathe

Scan your body.

Our first instinct is to touch our pain. It's ingrained.

Think about it. What do you do when your head hurts, or you stub your toe or your heart aches?

You touch your pain.

There is comfort in touch. It's an understanding. A togetherness. And it touches our true need.

But what if you can't feel it? What if all you feel is the pain, not the touch? Numbness can be physical and emotional.

Nudge the edges. As on the surface of a pond, allow the ripples to flow and intertwine. Touch and movement are not just in the physical body. Look deeper at the energy supporting it. Gently approach your resistance.

Little Guy, although numb and paralyzed, can move and feel even as he cannot.

The Danish have a word, Gennemleve. It means to live something through to its completion, to remain aware of and in contact with the process, and then, finally, to come to peace with it.

My perōrāre. My final sonnet. My conclusion meant to inspire you, my friend, is...

Our Final Flying Lesson.

Breathe as deeply as you can, today.

Our Flying Lessons

The Egg
Sometimes it's okay to step outside your skin.
Be willing to walk through hell.

The Eaglet
Find choice souls to hold it. Dogs work.
Be present in your skin.
Feel the triumph, no matter how small.

The Fledgling
Be honest with God.
Feel the pain, no matter how big.
Trust yourself.

The Eagle
Sometimes it doesn't change. That's okay.
Really live, now.
Breathe as deeply as you can, today.

About the Author

Angela Kari Gutwein is an artist and an Aerospace Engineer. Zephyr Jackson, her loyal Labrador, at her side, she lives and loves fully in the midst of suffering. She experiences the support and love of Jesus Christ in every intimate moment and in all of His creation. On her yoga mat, she soothes her nervous system, uncovering her true self. Angela sinks her fingers into the soil and into the written and spoken word, creating beauty.

www.theflyinglessons.com

Thank you so much for reading one of our **Biography / Memoirs**.
If you enjoyed our book, please check out our recommended title for your
next great read!

Z.O.S. by Kay Merkel Boruff

"...dazzling in its specificity and intensity."

–C.W. Smith, author of *Understanding Women*

CPSIA information can be obtained
at www.ICGtesting.com
Printed in the USA
FFHW012129180219
50586915-55944FF